KNOW YOUR
BIBLE
DEVOTIONS FOR KIDS

A. L. ROGERS

BARBOUR **kidz**
A Division of Barbour Publishing

ISBN 978-1-63609-608-7

Cover Design: Greg Jackson, Thinkpen Design

Published Barbour Publishing, Inc., 1810 Barbour Drive, Uhrichsville, Ohio 44683, www.barbourbooks.com

Our mission is to inspire the world with the life-changing message of the Bible.

Member of the
Evangelical Christian
Publishers Association

Printed in China.

001648 0723 HA

INTRODUCTION

**It's never too soon to know your Bible. . .
These devotions will make the learning fun!**

You want to learn new things and here's a great tool to help you know your Bible. These devotions address 101 topics vital to being a Christian, including

- knowing God
- faith
- prayer
- encouragement
- sin
- salvation
- loving your enemies
- and much more.

Written especially for 8–12-year-olds, these devotions offer you needed guidance for living, in a fresh and fun package. And each entry ends with references for further study, plus thought-provoking questions to help you interpret scripture for yourself.

You need to know your Bible. Make the learning fun with *Know Your Bible: Devotions for Kids!*

DEDICATION

To Jackson,
Matthew 5:16

READ GOD'S STORY

*How can a young man keep his
way pure? By living by Your Word.*
PSALM 119:9

What's your favorite book ever? Who are your favorite characters? You can probably imagine what they look like and how they would act if they were with you in person.

A helpful way to think about the Bible is like it's one big story. Chapters in a book are connected to tell a longer story. In the same way, the different books and stories in the Bible are connected to tell a longer story about God. God is the main character.

The Bible shows what God is like—who He is, what He cares about, and how He loves people, including you.

God's story is told by many different people over thousands of years. The Bible tells us in the book of Genesis how God created the world. Then, in the rest of the Old Testament (Exodus through Malachi), we see how He saved and taught the nation of Israel.

In the New Testament books of Matthew, Mark, Luke, and John, the Bible tells how God sent His Son, Jesus, to save people from their sin. And the story continues in the books of Acts through Revelation, showing how Jesus' followers shared this good news. They grew close to God and to each other.

That's where you come in!

This book will help you get to know God by reading the Bible. Like learning any good thing—playing an instrument or a sport, for example—that takes time and practice. Don't get discouraged if it's hard at first. Read God's story to know your Bible! The main character loves you, and He can't wait to spend time with you.

KNOW AND DO!

- Every chapter in this book has a Know Your Bible section with questions, prayer ideas, verses to read, or fun facts about God's world.

- Look at the Table of Contents in your Bible. There are 66 different books, divided into two parts. The Old Testament has 39 books. The New Testament has 27 books.

Meet the Trinity

May you have loving-favor from our Lord
Jesus Christ. May you have the love of God.
May you be joined together by the Holy Spirit.
2 Corinthians 13:14

When you play sports, it's important to use the right words. In soccer you don't score points, you score *goals*. This is because the ball goes into a large net called a *goal*. When you play baseball and softball, you score *runs*. This is because players have to *run* the bases in order to score. In basketball you shoot *baskets* to score *points*. Some baskets are worth two points and some are worth three. Do you see why it is important to use the correct words? The right ones help you understand what's really going on in a game.

That's true when we talk about God too. We need to use the right words to really understand Him. People often use the word *trinity* to describe God. This word means "three in one." The Bible shows us that there is only one true God (Deuteronomy 6:4–5). The Bible also shows us that God exists as three different "persons"—the Father, the Son (Jesus), and the Holy Spirit—and that each of these persons is fully God.

Are you confused yet? Don't worry if you are! Understanding that God is three in one takes time and prayer, and nobody will ever completely figure it out. But why do we need to know all of this anyway? Because knowing who God really is will help you understand His incredible love for you (John 17:3).

God is powerful and amazing. . .and sometimes a little hard to understand. But using the right words to talk about Him will help. Know your Bible, and get to know the three-in-one God!

KNOW AND DO!

- *Trinity* can be summed up by saying: (1) there is only one God, (2) He exists as three persons, and (3) each person is fully God.

- Read about the time Jesus was baptized in Luke 3:21–22. Notice that God revealed Himself through all three members of the trinity.

PRAYER

Do not worry. Learn to pray about everything.
Give thanks to God as you ask Him for what you need.
PHILIPPIANS 4:6

Have you ever played the Quiet Game? During that game, no one is allowed to talk. No one is allowed to sing, hum, or make noise. . .you're supposed to be as quiet as you can. The person who can stay quiet the longest wins!

The Quiet Game is fun. But if you're not playing the Quiet Game and you stop talking to other people, that's a problem. It's important to talk! Talking to your friends at school is fun. Talking to your parents makes you feel close to them. Talking kindly with your siblings or cousins will help you have good days together. Talking is one way we show love, ask for the things we need, and find help. It's also how we tell jokes, share stories, and encourage others. Talking is great!

Did you know that prayer is talking with God? When you pray you are speaking directly to Him. You can pray out loud or silently. You can pray with other people or by yourself. You can pray when you're scared, angry, happy, sad—any time. In prayer you can share with God every-thing, whether it's good or bad. Prayer is one way to grow close to Him.

Prayer is also responding to what God has said. The Bible is God talking to you. . .and when you pray, you respond to what He has said. Through prayer, you have a conversation with God.

In order to know Him and understand Him, we must pray regularly. Go ahead! Don't be afraid. You can start talking with God right now.

KNOW AND DO!

- Read 1 Thessalonians 5:17. How much should we pray?

- Jesus taught His followers how to pray in Luke 11:1–4.

Understand Sin

And the Lord God made clothes of skins
for Adam and his wife, and dressed them.
Genesis 3:21

———

The Bible's story of Adam, Eve, and the snake is important for many reasons. One important reason is that it shows us God's reaction to *sin*.

Do you know what sin is? Sin could be anything from stealing to being dishonest, from being selfish to hurting another person. People sin when they do something that does not please God.

The story of Adam and Eve shows the first sin in the Bible. The first two human beings chose to eat fruit from the one tree in the garden that God said to avoid. They listened to the tricky, lying snake instead of God. Adam and Eve knew they were wrong and tried to hide. But God found them. Then Adam blamed Eve and Eve blamed the snake. No one would admit to their own bad choices (Genesis 3:1–13)!

God reacted to this sin in two ways—with *punishments* and with *love*. Adam and Eve had disobeyed God, and there were consequences for their choices. So God punished them (verses 14–19). But God also loved them and gave them what they needed. Adam and Eve needed clothes and a new place to live right away to avoid bigger problems. So God made them clothes and sent them out of the garden of Eden (verses 21–24).

Since that time, every person has sinned. . .even your mom, your grandpa, and your favorite teacher. But God loves people anyway, so much that He made a way to save us from our sins. You'll learn more about that as you read this book.

Yes, there are consequences for sin. If you are caught cheating in school, you might fail a test or go to detention. But God still loves you. Sin is powerful, and tricky as a snake—but it cannot stop the love of God. Let's learn more about that love!

KNOW AND DO!

- Read the whole story in Genesis 3 with a parent, teacher, or friend. Pray about what you've read together.

- Read the devotion called "Know the Truth" (page 59) to understand more about sin and God's love.

THE GOOD NEWS

"For God so loved the world that He gave His only Son. Whoever puts his trust in God's Son will not be lost but will have life that lasts forever."
JOHN 3:16

Dale couldn't understand why Jesus was such a big deal. People at his church talked about Jesus all the time. They talked about "the good news of Jesus." They sang songs about Jesus. The pastor gave long, boring sermons about Jesus. Even in the kids' classes, all the teachers talked about was Jesus. Why is He so important? And what is this good news? Dale had a lot of questions.

The good news is that God has forgiven us of sin through Jesus. If we believe Jesus is God's son and ask God to make us right, He *will* forgive us—and we will live forever with God, even if our bodies die. This message is the good news! It is also called the *gospel*.

It's a lot to understand. Don't worry if you have questions about Jesus like Dale does. That's a good thing! God wants to answer your questions. This book will help you understand more about the good news of Jesus and guide you to answers in the Bible.

If you feel guilty about sin in your life, don't be afraid. Here is a prayer you can pray right now:

Dear God,
I know that I have sinned. Please forgive
me for the bad things I have done. Thank You
for sending Your Son, Jesus, to pay the cost
of my sin. Thank You for loving me!
Amen.

When you know your Bible, you'll know God's good news!

KNOW AND DO!

- Did you pray this prayer? If you did, find an adult who loves God and tell them about it.

- God loved *everyone* enough to send Jesus. No matter where you're from or what you look like. No matter what bad things you've done or what bad things someone has done to you—God loves you!

Know Your Name

For to us a Child will be born. To us a Son will be given. And the rule of the nations will be on His shoulders. His name will be called Wonderful, Teacher, Powerful God, Father Who Lives Forever, Prince of Peace.
Isaiah 9:6

Names are important. Have you ever thought about that? You're not just a random boy or girl. You're David, or Stephanie, or Devon, or Lilly! Names show the world how unique we are. You're not Stephen, you're Steve. You're not Candace, you're Candie.

Names sometimes connect you to your family history. Your name might be the same as one of your parent's. Or maybe your middle name is the same as a close family friend. Or maybe you have a name that your parents just really liked. In one way or another, your name tells a story about your family and about you.

The prophet Isaiah described Jesus—hundreds of years before He was born—through a list of powerful names:

- Wonderful
- Teacher
- Powerful God
- Father Who Lives Forever
- Prince of Peace.

Aren't those names incredible? Each one describes Jesus' goodness and power. They all connect Jesus to His Father, God, the creator of all that we see. These names give us confidence to worship and follow Jesus—He is the Powerful God!

So, what is special about your name? What story does it tell about you and your family? Talk to the Wonderful teacher about it today. Tell Him about your own name and thank Him for the story it tells. And remember the name He has given you: child of God (1 John 3:1).

KNOW AND DO!

- Read Isaiah 9:2–7. These verses are often read at Christmastime, but you can read them any time of year. It's always good to remember the names of Jesus.

- These verses in Isaiah are a *prophecy*, a word that God gave about the future. They were spoken over six hundred years before Jesus was born!

You Are the Image of God

Then God said, "Let Us make man like Us and let him
be head over the fish of the sea, and over the birds
of the air, and over the cattle, and over all the earth,
and over every thing that moves on the ground."
And God made man in His own likeness. In the likeness
of God He made him. He made both male and female.
Genesis 1:26–27

In the first chapter of Genesis, God created both animals and people. Some animals have hair similar to human hair. Some animals have teeth and eyes similar to people too. There are animals that eat fruits and veggies, drink cool water, and spend time together as families just like people do. So what makes us different?

The most important thing that separates people from animals is found in Genesis 1:26–27. These verses say that God made humans in His image. This means He set people apart from the rest of creation. He made people to be like Himself.

Some kids look like their parents. Leeland has his mom's wide smile. Peggy has her dad's brown eyes. In the same way, people share traits with God. For one thing, every person has an eternal soul just like He does—that means there is a part of us that will live forever. Because we are made in God's image, every single human life is valuable and should be treated with respect.

This idea of humans being made in God's image is something that really smart men and women have written whole books about. But it means something very important for you today: that you are precious to God.

Your life is more valuable than any amount of money, and more special than the most amazing gift. God set you apart from all of creation. He loves you deeply and shared His traits with you. Your life is a treasure!

KNOW AND DO!

- Read Genesis 1:28–31. What did God give people?

- Do you look like your mom or your dad? Do you think or sound or act like one of them? What traits do you share with your parents?

LOOK FOR RAINBOWS

"When the rain-bow is in the cloud, I will look upon it to remember the agreement that will last forever between God and every living thing of all flesh that is on the earth."
GENESIS 9:16

When it rains, clouds hide the light of the sun. The sky turns gray and ugly. Water falls to the earth, soaking everything it touches. The ground gets soggy, like a sandwich with too much jelly. Not many people enjoy the rain.

But when the sun starts to break through the clouds again, you might see something beautiful. The rays of light reflect off the water that's still in the air creating a rainbow. Have you ever seen one? A whole bunch of colors—from red to yellow to green to blue—can be seen in the shape of an arch. The ugly gray sky is brightened by bold colors.

A long time ago, God made a promise to a man named Noah. You remember Noah, right? He's the guy who built a huge boat to save his family and the animals of earth from a giant flood.

After that flood, God promised that He would never again destroy the whole earth with water. And God gave Noah something to help him remember the promise: a rainbow. God said that whenever He saw a rainbow, He would remember His promise not to flood the whole earth again (Genesis 9:14–15).

God has kept that promise. That's one of the wonderful things about Him—He is a promise keeper!

Next time you see a rainbow, you can think of God. He keeps His promises and makes beautiful things appear where there were once dark clouds.

KNOW AND DO!

- The story of Noah and the flood is in Genesis 6:1 through 9:17.

- Most rainbows can only be seen for a few minutes. But the longest-lasting rainbow ever recorded lasted 8 hours and 58 minutes!

Meet Abraham

Now the Lord said to Abram, "Leave your country, your family and your father's house, and go to the land that I will show you. And I will make you a great nation. I will bring good to you. I will make your name great, so you will be honored. I will bring good to those who are good to you. And I will curse those who curse you. Good will come to all the families of the earth because of you."
Genesis 12:1–3

Who was the first American? George Washington was the first president—was it him? Or was it Christopher Columbus, the explorer who sailed from Spain to North America? Or was it the Native Americans who lived on this land before Washington and Columbus? It's an interesting question, one we can ask about other countries too. Who was the first German, the first Filipino, or the first Japanese person?

The Bible is full of stories about a nation called Israel. This nation began when God made a promise to a faithful, obedient man named Abram. He was chosen to start a country that would worship God alone. Other nations would learn about God through Israel. Even today, we are learning about God—what He did, how He loves, what He expects—by reading the Bible's stories of Israel.

All of this started with Abram. God asked him to leave his home and move to a new land. God basically said to

Abram, "Trust Me!" Abram obeyed and it changed his life.

He wasn't a perfect man, just a regular person. But Abram put his faith in God. He did what God said, and he became an important character in God's story.

God still uses regular people to do amazing things. You don't need to be perfect for God to love you. He wants to bless you and change your life too. Put your faith in God like Abram did. Just see where He leads you!

KNOW AND DO!

- Along the way, God changed Abram's name to *Abraham*, which means "exalted father." He was the father of a nation—now that's one important dad!

- Read about Abram's name change in Genesis 17:1–6.

Let Your Light Shine

"Let your light shine in front of men.
Then they will see the good things you do
and will honor your Father Who is in heaven."
Matthew 5:16

———————

For as long as she can remember, Leah has been fascinated with lights. When she was little, she would turn the light switches on and off and on and off until it made her parents crazy. One day, her dad installed a lamppost at the end of their driveway. "So visitors will know where to turn," he said when Leah asked why. She also wondered about the bright spotlight above the front door. "This one shows our friends where to come in to the house," her dad explained. "We want to make sure they feel welcome."

Light sends darkness away. When it shines, people find the paths they should follow and the doors they need to walk through. Today's verse reminds us that when we turn on a light, it's best to lift it up high so everyone can see.

Did you know that you have a "light" inside you? The love of God is that light (Matthew 5:14–16)! Because God loves you, you can love others. Because God is kind and caring, you can be kind and caring too. Because you have been forgiven of your sin, you know how good forgiveness can be. You can forgive others when they hurt your feelings. *This* is how to shine your light in the darkness—by sharing the love of God with others.

You have something wonderful to share with people—light! Let everyone see the love of God in you! They will see the things you do and praise God.

KNOW AND DO!

- The speed of light is over 186,000 miles per second!

- Jesus said, "You are the light of the world." What else did He say you are? Read Matthew 5:13.

Find the Lost Coin

*"What if a woman has ten silver pieces of money
and loses one of them? Does she not light a lamp
and sweep the floor and look until she finds it?"*
Luke 15:8

———————

Have you ever lost money? It's not a good feeling. It takes work to earn money, and once you have it, it's hard to save. Money is *valuable*—it's worth a lot.

So many things cost money, like food, clothes, and things for school. And there are always things you want to spend your money on, like your favorite candy, a new video game, or going to a movie. So when you lose money, it feels really bad.

But it is an amazing feeling to *find* the money you lost. When you see the missing dollar bill behind the dresser, or the coins in the bottom of your backpack, it feels great! Your valuable money is found and can be used for something you want or need.

But what does this have to do with God?

Well, God loves it when people say they are sorry for their sin. And Jesus explained just how His Father feels by telling a story about a lost coin. You know how good it feels to find something valuable. . .and that's how God feels when you say you're sorry about a bad choice and begin to follow Him again. You are *valuable* to Him, and He is so pleased when He has you back safe and sound.

God's love is incredible. You don't have to be lost when He's always looking for you.

KNOW AND DO!

- Read the full story of the lost coin in Luke 15:8–10.

- Jesus often used stories to teach people about God. These stories are called *parables*.

LISTEN

Watch your steps as you go to the house of God.
Go near and listen but do not give the gift of fools.
For they do not know they are sinning. Do not hurry
to speak or be in a hurry as you think what to tell God.
For God is in heaven and you are on the earth. So let
your words be few. For a dream comes with much work,
and the voice of a fool comes with many words.
ECCLESIASTES 5:1–3

When Ryan goes to church, he hears a choir singing. They sway like trees waving in the wind. Sometimes the music gets so loud, Ryan thinks the roof is going to blow right off the building! It's all so joyful that Ryan is reminded of God's love.

At her church, Renee hears babies. Every Sunday she helps her grandma in the nursery. The babies coo and giggle as Renee tickles them and sings to them. They whine and cry when they want a bottle or need changed. All the sounds remind Renee that God loves families.

When Janet goes to church, she hears stories. Every adventure in the Bible interests her—Daniel and the lions, Esther and the king, Jesus and His miracles. Every story makes Janet more curious. After church, she re-reads the stories, just to make sure she didn't miss any details. And Janet is reminded that God is always doing something good with the people who follow Him.

Today's verses were written down by the wisest man who ever lived: King Solomon (1 Kings 4:29–34). If there was ever anyone who had a reason to talk, it was Solomon. But in these verses, he reminds us that it is important to *listen*.

Next time you go to church, pay attention to the words of the songs, the sounds of the people around you, and the stories in the Bible. As you listen, you might hear something that reminds you of God too.

KNOW AND DO!

- Sing the first verse of your favorite song from church. What do the words say about God?
- Read Proverbs 12:15. What do wise people do?

FAITH

*Now faith is being sure we will get what we
hope for. It is being sure of what we cannot see.*
HEBREWS 11:1

The Bible is full of amazing stories. There's the one about the huge flood and the ark that Noah built. There's the one about the shepherd boy David, who knocked down a giant with a sling and a stone. There's the one about Esther, who risked her life and saved her people. There's the one about Mary, who trusted God and gave birth to the baby Jesus. And there's the one about Jesus, who died on a cross and then rose again. And that's just a few of the amazing stories in the Bible.

All of them, in one way or another, help us see how powerful God is. Like the pictures we scroll through on a phone, each story shows God doing something incredible. But they show us even more than that.

The stories in God's Word show us what *faith* looks like. What is faith? Today's verse tells us that faith is "being sure we will get what we hope for" and "being sure of what we cannot see."

Part of following Jesus is putting your faith in God. This means that even though you can't see Him, you can believe He is real. Even though you can't see Jesus Himself, you can believe that he made the payment for your sins. Even though you can't see the Holy Spirit, you can believe that He is God, living inside you.

Faith in God is something that grows like a plant. Pray, read the Bible, and talk with other Christians about growing in faith. Give it a try, and see what happens!

KNOW AND DO!

- What's your favorite Bible story? Spend some time with someone you love and talk about it. Why do you like that story so much? What do you think it shows you about God?

- Read Hebrews 11:1–31 on your own or with a parent. Look at all the amazing ways God has blessed faithful people!

GO THROUGH THE ROOF

*"I say to you, 'Get up. Take your
bed and go to your home.'"*
MARK 2:11

Five men wanted to see Jesus. But there were two problems. First, there were so many people around that it was impossible to get to Jesus. Second, one of the five guys was paralyzed—he could not move his arms and legs.

So what did these men do? The four who were able climbed up on the roof of the building where Jesus was. As the people crowded Jesus like busy bees in a hive, the men made a hole in the roof above Jesus, then lowered their paralyzed friend on his bed mat. There, in front of everyone, Jesus performed two miracles: He forgave the man of his sins and then healed him. The paralyzed man picked up his mat and walked out of the house!

This amazing story never would have happened if those four men weren't such good friends. It must have been hard work to climb up on a roof, pull up their friend, and then tear a hole in the roof to get to Jesus. The sun in their eyes, the sweat on their faces, all the people staring at them. . .these men must have truly loved their paralyzed friend.

Can you be a true friend to someone? Can you think of someone that needs you to "carry their mat"? What can you do for someone else that will show them how much you care? Would you go so far as to lower someone through a roof to meet Jesus?

This is true friendship, and it honors God. Reach out and be someone's friend!

KNOW AND DO!

- Roofs during this time were made of mud plaster and thatch (straw).

- Read the whole story in Mark 2:1–12. What was the first thing Jesus did for the paralyzed man? Do you think this tells anything about what God sees as most important?

MEET MOSES

*The Lord saw him step aside to look. And God
called to him from inside the bush, saying,
"Moses, Moses!" Moses answered, "Here I am."*
EXODUS 3:4

———

Tammy loves to talk. She can talk for hours to *anyone* about *anything*. She talks on the bus ride to school, in between classes, and during recess—loudly. When she gets home from school, she tells her mom every detail of her day. Sometimes Tammy talks so much in class, she gets in trouble! She was born with what some people call "the gift of gab."

Not everyone is like Tammy. Some people are afraid to speak in front of others. That was the case with Moses—he just wasn't much of a talker.

Moses was a Jew who was raised in Pharaoh's palace in Egypt. While the rest of the Jews were slaves to the Egyptians, Moses lived a life of ease. But as he grew up, he no longer wanted to live with the special treatment other Jews didn't have. He left Egypt and lived in the wilderness. That's where God spoke to him and gave him a job to do: "Go speak to Pharaoh and free the Jews."

Sometimes God uses unlikely people to do His work in the world. When God needed a leader to tell Pharaoh to let the people out of slavery, He could have chosen a big talker. Instead, God chose a man who struggled to speak up. Why? Because Moses had faith (Hebrews 11:24–28).

God helps people to do amazing things they never thought they could do. What makes the difference? Faith in God's abilities, not our own. Learn to live as Moses did, with faith that God can use you.

KNOW AND DO!

- Read the amazing story of how God first spoke to Moses in Exodus 3:1–4:17.

- Are you a talker, like Tammy? Try to say something that shows your faith in God. Are you a quiet person? Ask God for the courage to do whatever He wants you to do.

LOOK OUT FOR OTHERS

*But the time came when [Moses' mother] could hide him
no longer. So she took a basket made from grass, and
covered it with tar and put the child in it. And she set
it in the grass by the side of the Nile. His sister stayed
to watch and find out what would happen to him.*

EXODUS 2:3–4

When Moses was a baby, a wicked pharaoh decided that
all Hebrew baby boys should be killed. Moses' mom had
to protect him! So she hid Moses in a basket and put him
in the river where he would float away. But Moses' older
sister followed along, watching over her baby brother.

Down the river, the pharaoh's kindhearted daugh-
ter found the baby. She quickly decided to raise him in
her palace. But she needed help. That's when Moses' sister spoke up. "I can find you someone to care for him,"
she said. Do you know who she found? Moses' own
mother!

The story of baby Moses is about God's goodness. He
watched over this little boy and gave Moses an amazing
part in God's big story many years later. But Moses' sister
also played a very important part. If she had not watched
over her baby brother, none of this might have happened.
Because she loved her brother, she helped to fulfill God's
plans for Moses.

Do you have a brother or a sister? Even if you don't,

you probably have cousins, friends, or neighbors. And you have Christian brothers and sisters—anyone who believes in Jesus like you do. Whoever is in your life, look out for them. Do your best to love them the way Moses' sister loved him, by watching over him when no one else could.

Think about it—God might use you to change someone's life!

KNOW AND DO!

- Lots of brothers and sisters argue—but try hard to love the ones you have. They are a special gift from God.

- How did the basket float? The Bible says Moses' mom used grass and tar to make it. Tar is thick and sticky and keeps water out. Moses' basket was waterproof!

See the Moon

*Then God made the two great lights, the brighter
light to rule the day, and the smaller light to
rule the night. He made the stars also.*
Genesis 1:16

The moon has always fascinated people, from scientists to astronauts to kids staying up after their bedtime. Here are some amazing facts about the moon you might not know:

1. The moon rotates (or spins) much slower than the earth does. So as it circles the earth, we always see the same side of the moon.

2. The moon does not create its own light. It just reflects the light of the sun back to earth.

3. The moon's gravity helps to smooth out the earth's, and it creates the ocean tides.

4. Twelve people and many more robots have landed on the moon's surface.

The Bible tells us some things about the moon too. It says that God created the moon on the fourth day and that He considered it "good." God made the moon so that there would be light even during the nighttime.

If you ever feel afraid of the dark, look for the moon. It may be high in the sky or close to the horizon. . .or it may not be in sight quite yet. But it will be, some-time soon. Remember that God created the moon to give the earth light. Like so many other things God has done, the moon is a reminder of His love for all of creation. You can enjoy that love, every time the moon is in the sky!

KNOW AND DO!

- One more amazing fact: the moon is 249,175 miles from the earth!
- The writer of Psalm 104 praises God for how He watches over creation. Read all of the psalm— or at least verses 18–24.

MEET DAVID

Then David said to the Philistine, "You come to me with a sword and spears. But I come to you in the name of the Lord of All, the God of the armies of Israel, Whom you have stood against. This day the Lord will give you into my hands. I will knock you down and cut off your head. . . . Then all the earth may know that there is a God in Israel. All these people gathered here may know that the Lord does not save with sword and spear. For the battle is the Lord's and He will give you into our hands."
1 SAMUEL 17:45–47

———

Most days are normal days. You go to school and spend time with your friends. You come home and hang out with your family. It happens again the next day.

But there are other days that change *everything*. The day your mom had another baby. The day your friend moved away. The day your favorite teacher retired. One of the most famous stories in the Bible is about a day that changed everything—the day David killed Goliath.

The Israelite army was facing the scary Philistines. The Philistines actually had a *giant* on their side named Goliath (verse 4). This huge warrior stood in an open field between the two armies, making fun of God and challenging the Israelites; but the Israelites were afraid. No one was willing to face the giant.

David was just a shepherd boy, visiting his older

brothers who were in the army. He hated to hear Goliath mocking God, so David volunteered to fight the giant. He had faith that God would win the battle for him.

It seemed like a crazy idea. Most people thought David was going to end up dead. Goliath was a trained fighter! He had a huge sword and he was twice David's size.

As the giant charged the boy, David put a stone in his shepherd's sling and flung it across the battlefield. That one little rock hit Goliath right in the head and killed him! Amazingly, David won the battle—and everyone was reminded of God's power.

God is still that powerful. And He'll use His power to help you!

KNOW AND DO!

- This was a day that changed everything for David, putting him on a path to become king of Israel.

- Read 1 Samuel 17:12. Where was David's father, Jesse, born? Can you think of a very important person who would be born there hundreds of years later?

KNOW THE PROMISE KEEPER

*Every good promise which the Lord had
made to the people of Israel came true.*
JOSHUA 21:45

"If you help me clean my room, then I *promise* I'll play a board game with you."

This was all Jenny needed to hear from her older sister Katherine. Jenny was only five, and she loved to hang out with her big sister. After Katherine made this promise, Jenny got to work immediately. She made the bed. She put books back on the bookshelf. She even dragged Katherine's basket of dirty laundry all the way downstairs to the washing machine. She was so excited to play a game with her sister!

The only problem was that Katherine didn't really want to keep her promise. So she made up excuses. "I need to finish my homework first." "I can play after this show is over." "I didn't necessarily mean we play right now." After a while, Jenny understood what was really happening. She left Katherine and went to another room, sad about the broken promise.

It hurts when people break promises. But the Bible tells us that God is quick to keep His! When God says He will do something, He does it. When God says He loves you, He means it. When God says He will always be with you, then you don't have to wonder if He's really there.

We can't control whether other people keep their promises. But we can trust in God, who always does what He says He will do. Know your Bible, and know the promise keeper!

KNOW AND DO!

- Read Joshua 21:43–44. These are promises God kept for His people, the nation of Israel.
- Is God slow or quick to keep His promises? See what 2 Peter 3:9 says.

LOVE THE LORD YOUR GOD

*"And you must love the Lord your God
with all your heart and with all your
soul and with all your strength."*
DEUTERONOMY 6:5

Think of the people you love most in the world. Your mom. Your dad. Maybe a brother or sister or friend. Your grandparents. Your cat or dog. (Okay, pets are not people. But still, they're just so lovable!)

Love is easy to understand. It's that strong feeling of affection for the people and things you like best. You just *feel* it. But sometimes it's hard to know how to *show* love. Today's verse is about loving God—how are we supposed to show love to *Him*?

Let's think about what makes other people feel loved. Moms and dads feel loved when kids listen and obey the rules, and when their kids are kind and caring. Friends feel loved when you talk and play with them. Brothers and sisters feel loved when you make time for them and build them up with kind words.

Today's verse was given to the nation of Israel by God Himself. Years later Jesus repeated the words to His followers (Matthew 22:37–38). Loving the Lord God is an important part of following Him. And we love God the same way we love others: We speak with Him (by praying)

43

and we listen to Him (by reading the Bible). We'll be sure to spend time with Him regularly.

Love the Lord your God. . .He loves you too.

KNOW AND DO!

- How can you love God today? By praying? By reading the Bible or serving someone else? Pick one of these ways and give it a try.

- Deuteronomy 6:6, the next verse after today's, says, "Keep these words in your heart that I am telling you today." Try to memorize today's verse and think about it often. That's how you can "keep it in your heart."

A Love That Covers Many Sins

*Most of all, have a true love for
each other. Love covers many sins.*
1 Peter 4:8

Nolan had bullied Robbie for years. Ever since they were in kindergarten Nolan had tried to control Robbie. Nolan liked to be in charge, to think that he was the coolest.

Sometimes Nolan was nice, but many times he made fun of Robbie to get others to laugh. Robbie didn't like it, but he didn't have other friends. He decided he would rather be with a mean Nolan than have no one to play with during recess.

Then the boys went to middle school and everything changed. Nolan suddenly got new friends. He wouldn't let Robbie sit at their lunch table or hang out with them. Nolan's words became especially mean too. Robbie felt hurt, angry, and lonely.

The only way Robbie could forgive Nolan was to love him the way God loves everyone. Robbie's parents taught him today's verse. They said, "Love covers many sins."

Robbie knew that God loved him very much—so much that He sent Jesus to pay the cost of Robbie's sins. Robbie decided that because God had loved and forgiven him, he should try to love and forgive Nolan.

Robbie slowly began to make new friends. He didn't talk to Nolan much, but when he did, he tried to be kind even if Nolan wasn't. It was hard, but with God's help, Robbie was okay.

Because he focused on God's love and tried to love in the same way, Robbie was able to rise above Nolan's selfishness. With God's help, you can too.

KNOW AND DO!

- Many people quote this verse by saying, "Love covers a multitude of sins." *Multitude* means a great number, or a lot.

- Has someone sinned against you? Can you try to love them the way God loves? Pray and ask.

MEET DANIEL

*Now God gave Daniel favor and pity
in the eyes of the head ruler.*
DANIEL 1:9

Do you know what it feels like to be different from everyone else? Do you know what it feels like to be somewhere you don't belong?

The Bible tells the story of a young man named Daniel. He was taken from his home in Jerusalem, then forced to live and work in a faraway place called Babylon. He didn't look like the Babylonians. He didn't understand their customs. He didn't worship their gods. Can you imagine how it felt to be so different?

Daniel had chosen to follow God no matter what. He had a chance to eat the Babylonian king's food, but he said no—because that would not honor God. Even though Daniel was far from home and many people around him were trying to fit in, he still acted the way that he knew would please God.

The Bible says that God "gave Daniel favor and pity in the eyes of the head ruler" (Daniel 1:9). God was with Daniel the whole time, loving and protecting him in Babylon.

Next time you feel alone or different, follow Daniel's example in following God! Live like he did by making choices that honor God even when other people don't.

Always remember—God loves you. He will be with you no matter what.

KNOW AND DO!

- Read all of Daniel 1 for the story of Daniel's capture. Notice how he was willing to follow and trust God even when he was surrounded by people who did not follow God.

- The name *Daniel* means "God is my judge." How do you think God judged Daniel's choices?

LOVING WORDS

Death and life are in the power of the tongue,
and those who love it will eat its fruit.
PROVERBS 18:21

Here's something interesting: the average human tongue has about 10,000 taste buds. These tiny bumps are what allow us to taste the sticky sweetness of ice cream or the salty snap of French fries. Without those little bumps, we wouldn't enjoy chocolate, pizza, cereal, or peanut butter nearly as much.

But the Bible tells us our tongues can do much more than just taste food. "*Death and life* are in the power of the tongue." How is that possible?

Think about it: Has anyone ever spoken mean, angry words to you, and you felt like you were dying inside? "You're stupid." "Shut up!" "I'm better than you," are things our tongues can say that hurt others. But loving words bring life to people—and they please God. So practice saying, "Thank you!" "Good job!" "I love you," and "I forgive you." These words are a great way to use "the power of the tongue" to bring life to others. Get good at it by praying and asking God for His help. He loves your prayers, especially when you want His help to do good.

When you know your Bible, you'll know how important loving words are. Be a brother, sister, classmate, or friend who shares life with your tongue. (And enjoy your taste buds too. You have 10,000 reasons to go find a tasty snack!)

KNOW AND DO!

- Psalm 55:22 says, "Give all your cares to the Lord and He will give you strength." When something makes you feel a strong emotion like anger, embarrassment, or sadness, then pray about what made you feel that way. Prayer is a great way to use your tongue.

- The 10,000 taste buds on your tongue are replaced by your body about every two weeks. That's about 20,000 taste buds a month, up to 240,000 each year!

Obeying Your Parents

Children, as Christians, obey your parents. This is the
right thing to do. Respect your father and mother. This
is the first Law given that had a promise. The promise is
this: If you respect your father and mother, you will live a
long time and your life will be full of many good things.
EPHESIANS 6:1–3

God loves families! In Ephesians 5 and 6 God tells us how families should work. Ephesians 6:1 tells us, "Children, as Christians, obey your parents. This is the right thing to do."

But it's hard to obey our parents all the time. Sometimes moms and dads ask us to do things we don't want to do. They ask us to turn off our video games. Or wash our hands before dinner. Or clean up our rooms. Or be nice to our siblings. Sometimes disobeying—doing whatever we want—sounds like more fun.

But God designed families to work a certain way *because He loves us and knows what's best*. Parents are supposed to be the family leaders who treat their kids with love. Kids are supposed to obey their parents and show them love right back. God isn't trying to ruin your fun—and neither are your parents! Good parents know what is best for their kids. God does too—and in His love, He wants both parents and kids to enjoy every day together.

Next time you obey, pay attention: Did your obedience make your mom's bad day a little easier? Did your obedience help your dad finish a job around the house? It may not always be what you want to do. . .but obeying your parents makes everyone's life a little better.

KNOW AND DO!

- The Bible has instructions for parents too. Ask your mom or dad to read Ephesians 5 and 6 with you. Pray together. Ask God to help you show love to each other.

- It's okay if your family isn't perfect. The Bible is full of stories about families with problems. Thank God today that He loves you no matter what—and He loves your parents too!

REMOVE IDOLS

*"Have no gods other than Me. Do not make
for yourselves a god to look like anything
that is in heaven above or on the earth
below or in the waters under the earth."*
EXODUS 20:3–4

There was a boy who loved trading cards. He spent all of his time thinking about them. He organized them and reorganized them, again and again and again, because he just loved looking at those cards! The colors, the characters, the stories on the cards, even the way they felt and smelled—everything about them captured the boy's attention. He couldn't think about anything else.

He wouldn't let his younger sister even look at the cards, and he was mean to her when she tried. Then he started keeping his cards in a secret place in his room so only he could find them. One day the boy even lied to his mom so he could spend her money to buy new cards. He was caught, and he felt awful because of his behavior. He knew he had disappointed his mom and disobeyed God. How had he gone so wrong?

Many stories in the Bible show us how things can keep us away from God. These objects are called *idols*. An idol is anything we focus on more than God. They can be video games, phones, new clothes, or even a friend you would do anything to impress.

But Exodus 20:3–4 is God's own command to keep our lives free of idols. To know and love God more, we need to find these troublesome things in our lives and remove them. Toss them out! Don't let anything stand between you and God.

KNOW AND DO!

- It's not wrong to like trading cards, phones, or video games. So when do objects become idols?

- Can you think of anything that stands between you and God? Something that distracts you from loving Him or loving others? Pray about it right now, asking for God's love and forgiveness.

MEET ESTHER

And the king loved Esther more than all the women.
She found favor and kindness with him more than all
the young women, so that he set the queen's crown
on her head and made her queen instead of Vashti.
ESTHER 2:17

In fairy tales, princesses often find themselves in danger, until they're saved by some amazing person or event. One princess was saved by her fairy godmother. Another was saved by a kiss from her prince. Another met a band of seven friendly dwarves who helped her find her way back to safety. Sometimes, the princesses even become queens by the end of the story.

In the Bible, you can read the real story (not a fairy tale!) of a woman named Esther. She became a queen, and God Himself saved her from danger.

Once upon a time, in a land called Babylon, the king wanted a wife. He looked at women across the land, hoping to find the most beautiful one in the whole kingdom. Finally, he chose a young woman named Esther to become his wife, the new queen of Babylon. The king thought she was very beautiful. He did not know Esther was a Jew who worshipped God.

But an evil man named Haman knew—and he hated the Jews. So Haman tricked the king into writing a law that would let him kill all the Jews. Esther could get in big trouble by going straight to the king for help. But she decided to trust God and tell the king everything. She asked him to stop Haman's plans. Esther risked her own life to save her people.

God saved the Jewish people through Queen Esther. The king's law was changed, and Haman was killed instead.

Esther was a young person who trusted God with her whole heart. And because she did, she accomplished something very important. You can do the same.

KNOW AND DO!

- Esther's story shows us that God sometimes puts us in just the right place, at just the right time, to help others. Read Esther 4:13–16.

- Before Esther became queen she went by a Jewish name: *Hadassah.*

WALK WITH GOD

*O man, He has told you what is good. What does
the Lord ask of you but to do what is fair and to love
kindness, and to walk without pride with your God?*
MICAH 6:8

―――――――

"But what am I supposed to *do*?" the boy asked his mom.

"Just go outside and explore. I can't say what you will find to do. But if you look around, you'll find it."

"But Mom—" the boy whined.

"Go." He knew the conversation was over by the sound of his mom's voice. So he went outside. Within a few minutes the boy was happily climbing a tree.

That boy's question is one that most Christians ask themselves over and over: *What am I supposed to do?* We want to know what God wants for our own lives.

As you get older, you'll probably ask yourself this question whenever you have a big decision to make. *Should I do what my friends are doing after school? Should I join the team? Should I try out for the band? What does God want me to do?*

It's good to ask God for direction. Psalm 25:4 says, "Show me Your ways, O Lord. Teach me Your paths." But God doesn't always give us a clear answer. Sometimes He gives us choices and allows us to do what we think is best.

Whenever you feel uncertain, read Micah 6:8 again. It tells what God wants us to do *all the time*, whether we're facing a big decision or just living out a regular day: Do what is fair. Love kindness. Walk without pride before God.

KNOW AND DO!

- Micah was a prophet in Judah (1:1). His name means "Who is like God?"

- Is there a specific thing that God wants you to do today? If you can't think of anything, what can you do that is fair and kind?

KNOW THE TRUTH

*For all men have sinned and have
missed the shining-greatness of God.*
ROMANS 3:23

You are a sinner. Everyone is. There's nothing you can do or say to hide this fact from God. At some point you've lied, stolen, said something hurtful, or done something you knew was wrong. Everyone has sinned. Even your mom and dad and pastor.

Being a sinner is sad. You probably didn't even need to read Romans 3:23 to know that you have a problem: *you are not like God!*

Why is it important to think about this? *Because when you do, you will begin to understand the love of God so much better.* When you know you're a sinner, the good news of salvation in Jesus is like a warm sunrise. Just like the cold and dark of night are chased away each morning by the sun, your sins are taken away by Jesus. When He died on the cross, He took all the punishment of your sins on Himself. Then Jesus showed that He is more powerful than sin and death when He rose from the dead.

Romans 3:23 doesn't have to be sad or shameful. This verse can be a reminder of God's love for you! When you understand the truth about yourself, you take the first step to being free from sin—you can ask God to forgive you through Jesus, knowing that He will.

Let this verse remind you of God's shining-greatness. He has the power to make sin vanish like darkness in the morning.

Know your Bible. Know the truth.

KNOW AND DO!

- It takes sunlight over eight minutes to reach the earth. That means when you feel the warm sunlight on your skin, it's already eight minutes old!

- In John 8:32 Jesus says, "The truth will make you free." Thank God for this! God loves truth and frees people from sin.

Turn on Your Flashlight

At one time you lived in darkness. Now you are living in the light that comes from the Lord. Live as children who have the light of the Lord in them.
Ephesians 5:8

What happens when you turn on a flashlight in the dark? You can see where you're going! You won't step on Legos or stub your toes on the chairs. The path to take becomes easy to see.

Plus, lost things are found. *There's the TV remote! How did it get behind the couch? There's my backpack! It was stuffed under the bed.* Light helps us find the things we need.

And when there's light, people are less scared. Darkness can make people feel alone or in danger. But a warm night-light or the glow from mom or dad's room makes us feel better when we turn out our lights for sleep.

When you follow Jesus' example of loving God and loving others, it's like you're shining a light in a dark room. Your life is like a flashlight in the dark! With your love and kindness, you can help other people find their way through bad days. By your generosity, you can help them find the things they need. By loving others, we "live as children who have the light of the Lord in them."

"Living in the light that comes from the Lord" also means God will help you see through the "dark" things in life—our own bad choices and the bad choices of others. Thank God for His light!

KNOW AND DO!

- Read Psalm 119:105. Reading the Bible regularly is a great way to let God's light into your life. Try to read at least a little bit every day!

- The first flashlight was invented in 1899. These battery-powered devices eventually replaced fuel-burning lamps and torches that created a flame for light. But many people around the world still call flashlights "torches."

MEET MARY

[Jesus'] mother said to the helpers,
"Do whatever He says."
JOHN 2:5

Claire has absolute trust in her mom. At three years old, though she can't explain it yet, Claire just knows her mom will take care of everything. If mom says she'll make lunch, then lunch will get made. If mom says Claire needs to wear a coat, the little girl knows it's cold outside. If something scares Claire in the night, she runs straight to her mom's bed. She knows she'll feel better in her mom's arms. This kind of trust is complete—nothing can shake Claire's confidence in her mom.

When Jesus first began teaching people about God, His Father, people wondered if they could trust His message. One way Jesus showed people they could trust Him was by performing miracles. The first miracle He did was to turn water into wine at a wedding.

One thing that makes this story so interesting is Jesus' mom, Mary. She trusted in her Son's teaching and power before anyone else. Before He turned the water into wine, Mary simply told the servants at the wedding, "Do whatever he tells you." She didn't need Jesus to explain His plans or show her what He had in mind. She just trusted completely in God's power.

Mary's simple statement is a good one for us to remember today. Do what Jesus tells you. You can trust Him.

KNOW AND DO!

- Read Luke 2:39–52 for a story about Mary and Jesus when He was only twelve years old.
- Changing water into wine is the first miracle of Jesus recorded in the Bible.

PRAISE IN THE MIDDLE

Then Mary said, "My heart sings with thanks
for my Lord. And my spirit is happy in God,
the One Who saves from the punishment of sin."
LUKE 1:46–47

———————————

Bridgette could tell her mom wasn't happy. Bridgette's little sister, Jessica, had been born too early. Doctors put Jessica in a hospital room with lots of machines connected to her tiny body by tubes. It was really scary.

Bridgette's family spent almost all of their free time in the hospital, hoping that Jessica would be okay. Everyone seemed sad. Or nervous. Or just *different* somehow. Bridgette's mom didn't seem like herself at all.

But Bridgette's mom got a little happier when they were in the car. She would put Christian music on the stereo and sing loudly as she drove. Bridgette's mom loved to sing. Now, even in the middle of hard times, she praised God.

In the Bible, in Luke 1, Jesus' mom praised God in the middle of a hard time. Mary was still just a young woman, not yet married to Joseph. God put the baby Jesus into Mary through the Holy Spirit (Luke 1:26–38). In that time, it was really tough for an unmarried woman to be pregnant. Some people probably made fun of her. . .some might even have wanted to hurt her.

But even though she was in the middle of a hard,

scary situation, Mary sang praise to God. And we can do that during hard times too!

Sometimes we have bad days. At other times, the bad things go on and on and on—maybe grandpa gets sick for months, or a mean kid at school won't leave you alone all year. In the middle of times like these, think of Jesus' mother, Mary. Praise God for who He is—and trust Him to help you through.

KNOW AND DO!

- Read all of Mary's song in Luke 1:46–55. She praised God for many things He had done for her and her people.

- Are you in the middle of a bad situation today? Take a minute to praise God for His goodness.

God's Free Gift

You get what is coming to you when you sin. It is death! But God's free gift is life that lasts forever. It is given to us by our Lord Jesus Christ.
ROMANS 6:23

God has given you an *amazing* gift. What for? To free you from sin.

Sin deserves punishment. Sin leads to death! Adam and Eve learned this when God punished them for disobeying Him (Genesis 3). And then God had to kill some animals to make clothes for Adam and Eve. They had never seen death before.

After that, every person and animal would die, all because of sin. The Bible is full of stories about how sin leads to death. Sometimes people died because of some really bad thing they did. But every person—even the ones who seem nice and good—will die. Because the Bible says every person sins (Romans 3:23).

The cost of sin is always death. You cannot do enough good things to pay for your sin. You can't buy your way out of sin or earn freedom from sin. We're all sinners, people who will "get what you have coming to you." But there is hope!

The good news is that when Jesus died on the cross, *He took the punishment of our sins so we wouldn't have to!* Jesus was perfect, the son of God who never, ever sinned

(1 Peter 2:21–22). He chose to die and take all the punishment of sin. And He offers you this salvation as a free gift . . .all you have to do is ask. This is truly good news!

Only the perfect, sinless Son of God could pay for everyone's sin. And we are all sinners. But Jesus offers us the gift of life that lasts forever—life with God, free from sin.

KNOW AND DO!

- Read Mark 10:17–22. This is the story of a rich man who wanted to earn God's free gift. What did Jesus say to him? "Come and follow me."

- Try to memorize Romans 6:23. Say it out loud every day. Share it with your family and friends.

YOUR REAL LIFE

"You have given me life and loving-kindness.
Your care has kept my spirit alive."
JOB 10:12

"How many times did you die before you killed the boss?"

"Like, six or seven."

"Did you level up?"

"Of course!"

When you're playing a video game there is always a way to get an extra life. Jump, hit the block, get the mushroom. One up! See the floating hearts? Run through them. Three more lives! Beat the boss at the end of the level with your best move (back, back, forward, A). You level up!

Have you heard of Job, from the Bible? If he was a video game character, he would have needed an extra life badly! But he was a real man, with real trouble. Job lost almost everything. Most of his family was dead. His money and his home were taken or destroyed. Even his health was bad.

But in all of Job's pain he said something powerful and true. More valuable than any smartphone or hard drive. More important than any video game. Job said God has "given me life." God "has kept my spirit alive."

Job reminds us that life is precious because it comes from God. A "life" in a video game is just one more try.

It's not a big deal. But real life is *a gift from God*. Your life is incredibly valuable. It comes directly from God Himself (Genesis 2:7).

Dive in to your real life! Spend time today doing things you can't do in a video game: Hug your mom. Thank your teachers. Ask a friend what's bothering her and listen—really listen—to what she says.

Thank God for the precious life you have, and live it!

KNOW AND DO!

- Take a break from screens with your mom or dad. Turn off the TV and the video games to talk and pray.

- Read the amazing description of God in Acts 17:24–26.

Your New Skin

Do not lie to each other. You have put out of your life your old ways. You have now become a new person and are always learning more about Christ. You are being made more like Christ. He is the One Who made you.
COLOSSIANS 3:9–10

In video games you can earn "skins" for your character. A new skin shows your character in cool new clothes, or a new haircut, or even with new powers. Some gamers buy new skins just for fun, changing them over and over. Characters can start to look like totally new people.

In some games you get to design your own character—one that represents you! You can pretend to be someone totally different from who you are in real life. Maybe you'll be a powerful wizard or a fearless dragon rider. Maybe you'll be a stealth ninja or a princess warrior. Maybe you'll have spiky instead of curly hair, or be tall instead of short. It's fun to get lost in another world for a while.

You can think of being a Christian in a similar way. But the "skin" you have as a Christian is a real, permanent change. Here's how the Bible describes it: "You have now become a new person. . . . You are being made more like Christ."

When you ask Jesus to forgive your sins—He does! And when you ask God to help you get over your hurts and grow stronger—He will! You are a *new person.*

Changing the skin on a video game character is fun, but it's just pretend. God has made you into a new person *for real.* This is so much more than a new look for a character. Check out your new, real-life skin!

KNOW AND DO!

- Have you ever made a bad choice that feels like the old version of you? Everyone does sometimes. Never forget that God will forgive you as soon as you ask. . .so ask!

- Did you know your skin is an organ, like your heart or lungs or brain? Skin is the largest organ your body has!

GOD'S GREATEST LAW

Jesus said to him, "'You must love the Lord your God with all your heart and with all your soul and with all your mind.' This is the first and greatest of the Laws. The second is like it, 'You must love your neighbor as you love yourself.'"
MATTHEW 22:37–39

It's hard for Jaime to make friends. He doesn't mind school. His teachers are nice to him. He's even pretty good at math and reading. But Jaime has a hard time with other kids.

Jaime just doesn't seem to fit in. Most of the kids ignore him. They don't want him to play with them during recess. Some of them are mean and make fun of the way he looks.

One day, though, Jaime's life at school changed. A new boy named Zach joined his class. They didn't become best friends right away, but there was something different about Zach. He talked to Jaime and treated him nicely. Zach said hello in the morning as they hung up their backpacks. Zach shared his pencil and book when Jaime forgot his. Zach never made fun of Jaime. After a while, they started to play together during recess. It made Jaime feel so good.

The Bible says that one day Jesus was asked, "What is the greatest law?" Jesus' answer can be said very easily: *Love God and love other people.*

Zach loved God. And he showed his love for God by showing love to Jaime. Zach didn't have to do anything hard or strange—he was just friendly and kind. Yet it made such a difference in another boy's life!

This is what God wants for every Christian. He wants us to love Him and to love others. Give it a try! It could change someone's life.

KNOW AND DO!

- What is one way people will know you're a Christian? Read John 13:35 to find out.

- Do you know anyone who doesn't have many friends? How can you show that person God's love this week?

WISDOM

*For the Lord gives wisdom. Much learning
and understanding come from His mouth.*
PROVERBS 2:6

———————

No matter how old you are, life is full of questions.

Should you take your new device to school or leave it at home?

Should you tell your mom about what happened on the bus or keep it a secret?

Should you do your homework before you watch TV or after?

How much candy and pizza should you eat at once?

In order to answer questions like these you need wisdom. But what's that?

When people are wise it means they can make good decisions. They think about what has happened in their lives before. . .and they learn from it. They listen carefully to others, so they learn from those lives too. They read the Bible so they can hear the words of God. Most of all, when they have decisions to make, they pray and ask God to help them make the best choices.

Life is full of questions and decisions. Kids need wisdom to make good choices just like adults do. Today's verses tell us "the Lord gives wisdom."

What choices will you have to make today? Do you have questions like the ones on this page? Whatever is happening in your life, pray about it today. Ask God to give you wisdom to make the best decisions you can.

KNOW AND DO!

- Who is the wisest person you know—the person who always seems to know the right thing to do? What can you learn from that person?

- To see what the Bible calls "the beginning of wisdom," look up Psalm 111:10 and Proverbs 9:10.

Follow What Is Good

Dear friend, do not follow what is sinful, but follow what is good. The person who does what is good belongs to God. The person who does what is sinful has not seen God.
3 John 11

Lisa didn't have many friends. She wanted to fit in at school so badly, and the other girls in her class seemed so cool. So when Denise made fun of the teacher, Lisa laughed with the group. When Jessica chased two girls away from her lunch table, Lisa said nothing. When Michelle started using cuss words, Lisa did too—even though she knew it was wrong. Pretty soon, Lisa was imitating *everything* the other girls did.

One of Jesus' disciples, John, wrote a letter to his friend Gaius. It's a short letter that focuses on right living. And in this short letter, John wrote down a powerful idea that God gave him: "Do not follow what is sinful, but follow what is good."

Lisa's desire to fit in was not wrong. Everyone wants to have friends. But she wanted to fit in to the group so badly that she imitated sinful behavior. The choices Lisa made were not pleasing to God.

Have you ever been tempted to act like Lisa? Is there a group of kids at school that tempts you to make bad choices? When you're with your friends this week, choose to make good choices. Be kind to others. Use words that are friendly and appropriate. See if you can get your friends to imitate *you*.

Always follow what is good.

KNOW AND DO!

- Third John is the shortest book in the whole Bible!

- Try reading John's whole letter at one time. It's just 14 verses long. Who did John tell Gaius to imitate? Why? (Look in verse 12.)

THINK OF OTHERS

Nothing should be done because of pride or thinking about yourself. Think of other people as more important than yourself. Do not always be thinking about your own plans only. Be happy to know what other people are doing.
PHILIPPIANS 2:3–4

Eli was very good at soccer. In fact, he was sure he was the best player on his team. . .and he told everyone all about it. It was easy for Eli to steal the ball from the other team, dribble to an open spot on the field, and kick a goal. Sometimes Eli's teammates called for him to pass the ball to them. But he would keep the ball to himself and score as many times as he could.

Soon, the other kids started calling Eli a "ball hog." They got tired of hearing him talk about how good he was. They didn't want to play with him any more. Why?

Eli was *prideful*. Pride is the sin of thinking you are more important than others. It leads us to treat people badly and to make selfish decisions. How do we avoid this sin?

The apostle Paul told Christians in the city of Philippi, "Be happy to know what other people are doing." That is something you can do easily!

What are your siblings or neighbor kids up to today? What do your parents want to do? What about your teachers? What's on their minds?

Spend your time thinking about what's going on in other people's lives. Find out if you can help them with anything. Spend time with them or do something nice that they'll enjoy. For example, if you're playing soccer, pass the ball to your teammates.

When you think of other people first, you begin to see how important they are—and you please God. This is the best way to avoid the sin of pride. Always think of others!

KNOW AND DO!

- Thinking of others as more important than yourself does not mean that you are not important. When everyone thinks of others as more important, then everyone feels important.

- Read Proverbs 16:18. What follows pride?

CONTENTMENT

Keep your lives free from the love of money.
Be happy with what you have. God has said,
"I will never leave you or let you be alone."
HEBREWS 13:5

———

Lydia loved the new blouse she got for Christmas—until she learned that her friend had gotten a new blouse and skirt. Lydia wished she had a new skirt too. Suddenly, she was unhappy, even though her old skirt was still very nice.

Mike loved his new video game. Then he saw commercials for a new controller and a carrying case. Soon, all Mike could think about was how much he wanted those things too. He wanted them so badly he didn't even enjoy the game he had.

Lydia and Mike are having trouble being *content*. Contentment is being thankful and satisfied with what you have. Lydia and Mike might still want new clothes and video game accessories. But if they were content, they wouldn't need those things to feel happy. Instead, they would be thankful for what God has given them. They would happily enjoy what they have, without complaining about things they don't.

God tells us in Hebrews to "be happy with what you have." This is a wise way to live. When you choose to be content with what you have, you free yourself from envy and selfish choices. Make the choice to be content! It helps you to feel closer to God and to enjoy other people.

KNOW AND DO!

- Practice contentment by praying about all the things you have and love. Thank God for your favorite things. Ask Him to help you be satisfied with them.

- Sometimes we lose or break the things we love. When this happens, we can still choose to be content with God's love. He says, "I will never leave you or let you be alone."

Hold On to What You've Been Taught

So then, Christian brothers, keep a strong hold on what we have taught you by what we have said and by what we have written.
2 THESSALONIANS 2:15

In the school cafeteria, a boy told Danielle that "praying before you eat is stupid."

Another time, at a sleepover, Danielle's friends made fun of her because she wouldn't watch a bad movie.

And on another day, a kid on the bus said Jesus was fake and God wasn't real. The boy made fun of Danielle for believing.

Unfortunately, you will meet people who make fun of you for being a Christian. People often make fun of things they don't understand. It helps them feel smarter and less afraid of the things they don't know about.

Today's verse reminds us to hold on to what we've been taught. When someone challenges your faith or makes fun of you for following Jesus, pray silently to God. Ask Him to help you hold on to the things you know are true. Ask Him to help you make the best decisions you can.

God has chosen *you* to share the good news of Jesus with the people around you (2 Thessalonians 2:14).

Sometimes the best way to do that is simply by being kind—by making the choice that pleases God right in front of them.

That isn't always easy to do—especially when someone is making fun of you—but with God's help you can. And no matter what, God is always with you.

Know your Bible. Then hold on to what you've been taught.

KNOW AND DO!

- Read 2 Thessalonians 2:16. Who loves you? Who will comfort you?

- Have you ever been mocked for making a good choice? Talk about this with a parent, a teacher, or a friend that you trust.

ONE GOOD QUESTION

One thing I have asked from the Lord, that I will look for: that I may live in the house of the Lord all the days of my life, to look upon the beauty of the Lord, and to worship in His holy house.
PSALM 27:4

Everyone asks questions. Your teacher asks for your attention. Your mom or dad asks you to help with dinner. Your friend might ask to borrow a pencil, and the bus driver might ask you to sit down. How many questions do you think get asked in a day? It's probably a lot!

Questions are everywhere. And here's another one: How many questions do you ask God each day? Things like,

Will You make it stop raining?

Why do I have to go to school?

Will You please heal my grandma?

David, the writer of Psalm 27 says, "One thing I have asked from the Lord." Just one? This must be important! What is it? "That I may live in the house of the Lord. . . and to worship."

If you could ask God for just one thing, would you ask to live in His house? Probably not. But David understood that to be close to God—to be in His "house"—is the greatest thing in the world. David also understood that worshipping God is how we can get close to Him.

We will not always have our questions answered. Sometimes we don't get what we want. When your friend doesn't loan you what you need or when your grandma doesn't get well, worship God anyway. In His house you will "see the loving-kindness of the Lord" (Psalm 27:13).

KNOW AND DO!

- To worship God means to show love, respect, and honor to Him.

- Try to figure out how many questions you ask your mom or dad in one day. Keep track on a piece of paper. You will be surprised by how many questions you ask!

AVOID BAD CHOICES

Happy is the man who does not walk in the way sinful men tell him to, or stand in the path of sinners, or sit with those who laugh at the truth. But he finds joy in the Law of the Lord and thinks about His Law day and night. This man is like a tree planted by rivers of water, which gives its fruit at the right time and its leaf never dries up. Whatever he does will work out well for him.
PSALM 1:1–3

———————

Elsie felt bad after she played with Danny. He made fun of everyone at school, calling them names or mocking the things they did. Sometimes he wasn't even nice to Elsie while they were together. It was like she had to be extra cool in order for him to be nice to her.

But when Elsie hung out with Mara, she felt great. Mara was kind. She would play with anyone at recess. She would eat lunch with anyone. Mara just loved to laugh—about the games at recess, someone's knock-knock joke, even the mistakes she herself made. When Elsie was with Mara, she laughed a lot too.

Today's verses are a warning. They tell us not to make the same bad choices that other people make. They also show us what it's like when we make choices that please God.

The Bible says that when we follow God's ways, we are like trees planted by living water—trees that are full of fruit. Have you ever seen an apple tree filled with red, juicy fruit? Lots of people can eat delicious apples from the same tree. This is what good choices are like—fruit everyone can enjoy!

You probably know people like Danny and Mara. Who will you choose to be like? Know your Bible, and avoid the bad choice.

KNOW AND DO!

- Psalm 1:1 says not to "stand in the path of sinners." Did you know that you use 100 different muscles when you stand up? Use those muscles for better things!

- Try to memorize Psalm 1:1. Focus on these three words: *walk*, *stand*, *sit*.

ENJOY THE SNOW

Take away my sin, and I will be clean.
Wash me, and I will be whiter than snow.
PSALM 51:7

Snow fell overnight and covered everything in town. It looked like a thick layer of frosting had been put on the world, and every building was a gingerbread house. Every tree branch and blade of grass was a strange new dessert, covered in sparkling white.

The sunlight reflecting off the snow was so bright it was blinding! When the townspeople came out of their homes, they had to wear sunglasses. It was like the whole world was shining back the light of the winter sun.

Today's verse describes what it's like when God forgives you of sin. It's like you've been washed "whiter than snow." There are no dark spots. There is no sin left over. God's love is big enough and powerful enough to forgive *everything*—like a big snowstorm covering every bit of the ground.

No matter what you've done, no matter what has been done to you, God can and will forgive. Just pray and ask! His forgiveness covers you completely, washing you as white as the snow.

KNOW AND DO!

- Lots of snow falls on planet earth each year. Imagine a one followed by fifteen zeros. That's how many cubic feet of snow falls in one year!

- You can reflect the love of God the way snow reflects the sunlight. How? By loving other people and forgiving them if they hurt you. Be so kind that they need to wear sunglasses around you!

ENJOY THE RAIN

"I will give you rain at the right time. So the land will give its food and the trees will give their fruit."
LEVITICUS 26:4

At the window, the raindrops seemed to be having a conversation. Each of the thousands of little drops that hit the glass had something to say. The raindrops were busy as bees making honey, and their sound was cheerful.

The earth needs rain. Plants and trees must have water to grow. Animals need to drink water from the rivers and lakes. The clouds hold the moisture that builds up in the air until the proper time, then drop their load as rain.

Rain is one way God takes care of the earth—and all of us too. Even though thunderstorms can sometimes be scary. Even though rain sometimes stops us from playing outside. Rain is actually a gift.

In the Bible, as the Israelites were moving into a new land, God promised to take care of them. He said He would send rain so the people's food and trees would grow.

This same God loves and cares about *you* too. Next time you eat an apple, a banana, or an orange, think about rain. God made that fruit grow with rain. He uses the rain to feed you! What a gift. Step outside and enjoy the rain!

KNOW AND DO!

- Read Leviticus 26:1–13. Notice all the ways God promised to take care of His people in their new land.

- Did you know that raindrops break into smaller drops as they fall? Some of the small drops that hit the sidewalk were once part of much bigger drops up in the clouds!

REMEMBER WHAT HE HAS SAID

*"He is not here. He is risen. Do you not remember
what He said to you when He was yet in Galilee? He said,
'The Son of Man must be given over into the hands of
sinful men. He must be nailed to a cross. He will rise again
three days later.'" They remembered what He had said.*
Luke 24:6–8

Have you ever attended a funeral? It's a sad time, isn't it? Imagine how the followers of Jesus might have felt after He died. Sad that He was dead. Angry at the soldiers who beat Him and hung Him on the cross. Perhaps confused, or even a little scared that they might be killed next. (They were Jesus' followers after all!)

After Jesus died, some of His followers visited His tomb. These women brought spices with them. It was the custom in that time to honor a dead loved one by spreading spices on the body. This would help to limit the smell of death.

But during this hard, emotional time, the women were visited by two angels. The angels told the women that Jesus is risen from the dead! The angels also reminded the women of things Jesus had told them. And the Bible tells us, "They remembered what He had said."

When you are feeling strong emotions—sadness or anger, confusion or fear—remember what God has said to you:

"I love you" (John 3:16).
"You are my child" (1 John 3:1).
"You are forgiven" (Luke 24:47).

You can trust God, even when you feel bad. When life is hard, remember the things He has said.

KNOW AND DO!

- Who were the women in this story? Read Luke 24:10 to find out.

- Ask your mom, dad, or one of your grandparents to show you some spices in the kitchen. Carefully smell them. Which ones smell the best to you?

MEET PAUL

All who heard him were surprised and wondered.
They said, "This is the man who beat and killed
the followers in Jerusalem. He came here to tie the
followers in chains and take them to the head religious
leaders." But Saul kept on growing in power. The Jews
living in Damascus wondered about Saul's preaching.
He was proving that Jesus was the Christ.
ACTS 9:21–22

―――――――

Have you ever made a bad choice and done something you knew you shouldn't have? Did you ever feel like you weren't good enough to be forgiven? Maybe you thought, "God can't love me anymore. I do too much bad stuff."

Well, meet a man named Saul. Saul had a long list of terrible things he'd done to hurt Christians. He was even on a mission to *kill* them. That's exactly the kind of person who could never be forgiven by God, right? Wrong. As we see in Acts 9:1–31, Saul's life was completely changed.

Jesus got Saul's attention as he was traveling to a city called Damascus. A light from heaven shone so brightly that Saul was blinded. Jesus told Saul that he had new work to do. After three days God sent a Christian named Ananias to care for Saul. Saul's sight came back, and God filled him with the Holy Spirit. This was an incredible act of forgiveness!

The story of Saul—soon to be known as Paul—continues through the rest of the New Testament. God not only forgave Paul but also gave him a very important job. Paul went from killer to missionary.

Enjoy forgiveness from God—like Paul did! God's forgiveness frees you of the shame of your sin. And God's forgiveness reminds you of the mission He gives to every Christian: to tell others the good news about Jesus.

KNOW AND DO!

- Nothing you can do is so bad that God will not forgive you. An Old Testament prophet named Micah reminds us God "is happy to show loving-kindness" and that He "will throw all our sins into the deep sea" (7:18–19).

- If you've done something bad, pray about it right now. Tell God what you've done and ask for forgiveness. Then join His mission—tell others that God has forgiven you of sin.

JOY

My Christian brothers, you should be happy when you have all kinds of tests. You know these prove your faith. It helps you not to give up.
JAMES 1:2–3

━━━━━━━━━

What are the things that make you happy? A brand-new bag of potato chips? A cold, bubbly soda that tickles your tongue? Maybe some extra screen time from mom and dad? Reading a favorite book or winning a game?

All of these things are great. They can make you happy for a while. . .but they don't last very long. Those new chips may be deliciously crunchy, but soon the bag is empty. Extra screen time is fun, but eventually your time runs out and you have to turn it off again. The things that make us happy are often *temporary*—that means they don't last forever. But things are different with something called *joy*.

Joy lasts longer than the things that make you happy. It's different. You don't have to have snacks or screen time to feel joyful. You don't have to win every game you play in order to have joy. Joy is knowing that God loves you no matter what happens, good or bad. Joy is feeling peaceful and glad because you can trust God with every part of your life. You can be joyful even when things go badly.

Have you ever visited someone who is sick in the

hospital? Sometimes they're more joyful than ever, because they know God is caring for them. Have you ever talked with someone after something really bad had happened? Sometimes, instead of feeling angry or scared, they are kind and forgiving, trusting that God will take care of them. *This* is joy.

KNOW AND DO!

- Joy is one of the fruits of the Spirit, found in Galatians 5:22–23.

- Why do you think Christmas songs mention joy? Talk about it with your parents. How did Jesus bring joy to the world?

PEACE

*"I have told you these things so you may have peace
in Me. In the world you will have much trouble.
But take hope! I have power over the world!"*
JOHN 16:33

May 8, 1945, is one of the most important days in history.
It is called V-E Day, which stands for "Victory in Europe."

That was the day Nazi Germany surrendered to the
countries it was fighting, including the United States
and England. V-E Day marked the end of World War II in
Europe, and the restoration of *peace*—no more fighting
after one of the worst wars that has ever been fought.
Peace means many things, including freedom, security,
and quiet.

Before He died on the cross to pay the cost of people's sins, Jesus talked about peace. He knew He was
going to die soon, and He knew that was hard for His
followers to understand.

So in John 16 Jesus explained many things about His
death and what would happen afterward—including the
Holy Spirit's coming to earth.

Jesus said all of this so that His followers would have
peace. They were not at war, like so many countries were
during World War II, but they were going to face many,
many hard days after Jesus' death. The ancient world
was very unkind to Christians. Jesus wanted them to feel

peace inside their hearts and minds—to enjoy strength in His love and freedom from sin—even during hard days. So He reminded them of something that is still true today. Jesus said, "Take hope! I have power over the world!"

What Jesus told His followers two thousand years ago, He tells you today. Take hope—you can have God's peace any time!

KNOW AND DO!

- What makes you feel angry or scared? What do you worry about? Pray about those things. Ask God to help you feel His peace even when life is hard.

- Philippians 4:7 is a famous verse about peace. Read it with your parents. Try memorizing it together.

GENTLE ANSWERS

*A gentle answer turns away anger,
but a sharp word causes anger.*
PROVERBS 15:1

Avery was one year older than Gabe. They were brothers, but they were very different. Avery was good at many things that Gabe was not. Avery could play basketball and soccer much better than his younger brother. He dribbled circles around Gabe on the court and on the field.

But Gabe seemed to get high grades without even trying. He would finish his homework half an hour before Avery did. Gabe was good with words in a way his older brother was not.

The two brothers fought the way brothers do, even though their parents disliked it. When Avery would get mad, Gabe faced a choice. On the one hand, he was smart enough to think up a really good insult—one that stung like a bee—which would really make Avery angry and probably get him in trouble with mom and dad. On the other hand, Gabe could use his ability with words to say something gentle and help his brother calm down. That would be like turning off an alarm before it rings and wakes everyone in the house.

Gentle answers are kind, calm, loving words. They help people to calm down instead of making them angrier. Gentle answers stop arguments rather than making them worse. The Bible says that gentle answers "turn away anger."

Do you know certain words and tones that make your siblings or parents especially angry? Next time you are tempted to use them, try a gentle answer instead! Show love by answering your family with kindness, in a calm voice. Gentle answers help people to have good days together.

KNOW AND DO!

- Read Proverbs 15:4. What is a "gentle tongue" like?

- Write down a list of gentle things you can say to your family. Try to say one every day.

BE A DISCIPLE

*[Jesus] went up on a mountain and called
those He wanted. They followed Him.*
MARK 3:13

Jesus had many followers, including both men and women. He also created a special group of twelve followers, often called the disciples. They followed Jesus on His travels and listened to His teaching more closely than anyone. Mark 3:13–19 includes the names of these twelve men.

A disciple is anyone who listens to a teacher and believes that the teacher knows what is best. Disciples then try to share their beliefs with others. (In case you're wondering, *disciple* isn't a word that is used with students and their teachers at school—you're not a disciple of your math teacher, even if she's cool.) Today, *disciple* is a word often used to describe the followers of someone who teaches about God.

You can be a disciple of Jesus today. All you have to do is *follow* Him. Following Jesus' teaching means a lot of different things. First, it means you believe God has forgiven you of your sins and that Jesus is God's Son. It also means you do your best to make good choices. It means that you keep learning about God by reading the Bible, praying, and asking God for help when life is hard. And most importantly, being a disciple of Jesus means that you love God and other people (Mark 12:30–31).

Being a disciple of Jesus will help you grow close to God. Does that sound exciting? Start following Him. Be a disciple today!

KNOW AND DO!

- Read Matthew 28:19. What does Jesus ask His disciples to do? How can you do this too?
- Jesus' disciples followed Him on foot or by riding on animals. They had lots of time to talk and have fun as they traveled.

COMMUNITY

*Work hard to live together as one by the help
of the Holy Spirit. Then there will be peace.*
EPHESIANS 4:3

The first person to walk on the moon was an astronaut named Neil Armstrong. As he took his first step in the moon's silvery dust he said, "That's one small step for a man, one giant leap for mankind." This moonwalk wasn't just for one man to enjoy. Neil Armstrong was part of a larger group of people—a *community*—called "mankind." That means every person around the world! It took thousands of hardworking people to get Armstrong safely to the moon. And all the people on earth would benefit from what he learned on his trip. Neil Armstrong understood that his actions affected other people, not just himself.

The same is true for you. Your actions affect other people, people who are part of communities. Your family is a community. The other kids on the school bus are a community. Your class at school is a community. Your sports teams and your church groups are all communities. In each of these places you will make decisions that affect others.

If you make fun of people or treat them rudely, you will hurt feelings. That affects everyone around you. Taking food or money or things that don't belong to you hurts other people too—no one likes to have their things taken. When you make a bad choice in community, it's like dipping a messy paintbrush in a clear cup of water. The paint spreads through the water, making the whole cup dirty.

But just like bad choices can affect a community, so can good ones! So think about your community today. Be sure to show others the love of God.

KNOW AND DO!

- If you aren't sure how to act in a community, ask God to help you make good choices. You'll begin to see how your actions affect others.

- Reads Acts 4:32. This is how the first Christians lived in community.

SELF-CONTROL

*A man who cannot rule his own spirit is
like a city whose walls are broken down.*
PROVERBS 25:28

Imagine living in an ancient city—like the ones we read about in the Bible. Your city is surrounded by a thick wall made of wood and stone. It stretches high above your head. Every night, large gates are closed to keep out enemies who might want to attack in the dark. Families sleep in houses inside the city wall. If there's enough room, even animals and crops are kept inside the wall.

The most important thing about the wall is that there can be no gaps in it—no gates left open, no broken-down sections. The wall has to completely surround the city for it to provide protection.

If you were an ancient city, the wall that would protect you is *self-control*. Having self-control means that you make good choices. When you are tempted to do something wrong, you are able to stop yourself and make a better choice. Even when you feel an urge to do something—whether it's good or bad—you don't have to do it to be happy. You have control over your words, your body, and your actions.

The Bible says that a person without self-control "is like a city whose walls are broken down." That's when enemies can climb inside. The city is not safe and secure.

Losing control of yourself leaves you in a dangerous spot too. When you don't have self-control, you let bad choices into your life—and they can hurt you.

So know your Bible and know self-control! It's a "fruit of the Spirit" (Galatians 5:22–23), one of the good things God grows in your life when you follow Jesus. Self-control is a great way to take care of all that God has given you. And it's a wonderful way to show love to others too.

KNOW AND DO!

- Practice self-control by counting to five slowly when you are angry. Then, calmly, talk about the problem.

- Beavers build dams—like those ancient city walls—which surround and protect them. You can be like a beaver!

LOOK TO JESUS

But when he saw the strong wind, he was afraid.
He began to go down in the water. He cried out,
"Lord, save me!" At once Jesus put out His hand and
took hold of him. Jesus said to Peter, "You have so
little faith! Why did you doubt?" When Jesus and
Peter got into the boat, the wind stopped blowing.
MATTHEW 14:30–32

For the disciples, following Jesus around was easy, right? After all, He could perform miracles and heal people. They probably had fun every day, right?

Well, maybe not.

In Matthew 14:22–33 the disciples are in a boat on a dark, windy night. The sea is tossing the boat like it's a little toy in a giant bathtub. The boat might turn over in the water, and the disciples could drown. Jesus, though, is still on shore. Late in the night He approaches them by performing a miracle: He walks across the water as if it is dry ground! The disciples are afraid, but Peter jumps out of the boat to go see Jesus.

It's amazing—as Peter looks at Jesus, he is able to walk on the water too. But then Peter begins to doubt Jesus' power. Suddenly, he starts to sink! But Jesus quickly pulls Peter out of the water.

It can be hard to trust God when bad things happen. When someone hurts you, or when someone you love has a problem, you might feel like you're sinking in a dark, windy sea.

But looking to Jesus is the best thing you can do. This means praying about the problem, talking with others who love Jesus, and trusting God no matter how bad things get.

Life is "windy" with problems. We can't control everything that happens to us. But Jesus will keep us from sinking. Always look to Him!

KNOW AND DO!

- Next time it is windy and rainy, ask your parents if you can go outside for a few minutes. Let the rain hit your face and feel the wind on your hands. Imagine what Peter saw and felt on that windy sea.

- The fastest wind ever recorded was 253 miles per hour! It was part of a tropical cyclone named Olivia in 1996.

Enjoy Your Sleep

Listen, He Who watches over Israel
will not close his eyes or sleep.
Psalm 121:4

Have you ever laid in bed awake for a long time, unable to sleep? The seconds seem to last for minutes, and the minutes seem to last for hours. It seems like the whole world slows to a turtle's pace—like the night is going to drag on forever.

Some people can't sleep when they've had too much junk food. Others can't sleep because they took a big nap earlier in the day. But the writer of Psalm 121 couldn't sleep because he was afraid and worried. Have you ever felt like that?

When kids are afraid and can't sleep, most of them will get out of bed in the middle of the night and wake up their parents. Every kid likes to have mom or dad wait by their bedside until they can fall asleep. Psalm 121 says that God cares for us like that. He is like a parent who waits by your bed, reminding you that you are safe, helping you to fall asleep.

If you're worried or afraid about something, talk with your mom or dad. And pray about how you feel. Don't be afraid to tell God what's on your mind. "The Lord watches over you" (Psalm 121:5). Roll over and enjoy the sleep!

KNOW AND DO!

- Pray to God every night before you go to bed. Ask one of your parents or a sibling to pray with you. Talk to God about your day and thank Him for watching over you.

- Did you know that most kids need between 8 and 10 hours of sleep every night? Better get your rest!

Do You Have Beautiful Feet?

How beautiful on the mountains are the feet of him who brings good news, who tells of peace and brings good news of happiness, who tells of saving power, and says to Zion, "Your God rules!"
Isaiah 52:7

There's nothing like getting a new pair of shoes. The colors are as bright as a new box of crayons. The sides and soles are so clean that you step carefully around anything that might make them dirty. New shoes make your feet happy!

Today's verse is about feet, which is kind of strange, isn't it? People in the Bible didn't have shoes like we do. So how could they have beautiful feet? What does this verse mean?

Isaiah 52:7 is about God saving the people of Israel from their enemies. The feet in this verse are "beautiful on the mountain" because they were a sign that good news was coming. The person making the hard trip across the mountain was telling everyone that God would keep His promise to save Israel from danger.

So what does this verse mean to us today? Well, God hasn't changed. He still keeps His promises, including His promise to save people from sin (Romans 10:13).

Can your feet be beautiful too? Can you share the good news about God's love with someone you know?

The best way to share that good news is by showing love to others—by being kind, by helping people, or by just spending time with them.

Your feet will take you lots of places. Wherever they take you, share God's love with others!

KNOW AND DO!

- Why did God save Israel from its enemies? Read Isaiah 52:10 to find out.

- The man with the world record for the largest feet on earth needs to wear a size 26!

Follow the Shepherd

The Lord is my Shepherd. I will have everything I need.
PSALM 23:1

―――――――――――

Sheep do best when they have a shepherd to watch out for them. A shepherd will lead his sheep to green fields where they can eat grass. He will also lead them to streams of clean, cool water so they can drink. At night, he'll lead the sheep into a pen—an area surrounded by a fence—so they can sleep without fear of danger. If a wolf or a bear ever surprises the flock, the shepherd is there to fight it off. Shepherds also shear sheep, which is like giving them a haircut. The shepherd cuts off the sheep's wool so people can make cloth. And the sheep are cooler and more comfortable as their wool grows in again.

Psalm 23 says we can think of God as our shepherd. We can count on Him to lead us to the things we need. This means more than just food. It includes the people who will help you grow into a kind and loving adult—like family members who love you and friends you can trust.

We can also trust in God the way a sheep puts confidence in its shepherd. God is our protector from dangers. This doesn't mean that bad things will never happen to us. Wolves still attack flocks of sheep, even when the shepherds are around. But it means that if something bad happens, you can count on God to be there, to comfort

you, to help you through the problem.
    Don't be afraid. Just follow your shepherd!

KNOW AND DO!

- Read John 10:14–16. How did Jesus describe Himself?

- We use wool to make yarn and clothing. One pound of wool can make almost 10 miles of yarn!

Be Prepared

Your heart should be holy and set apart for the Lord God. Always be ready to tell everyone who asks you why you believe as you do. Be gentle as you speak and show respect.
1 Peter 3:15

If you're going camping in the woods, you need to be prepared. You need to bring food to eat and a tent to sleep in. You need to pack the right clothes for the weather and maybe some bug spray to keep the mosquitos away. You might need a backpack, hiking boots, and a map. You don't want to be unprepared when you go camping. That's how people get lost or hurt in the woods!

Jesus' disciple Peter told Christians to be prepared—but not for a camping trip. He wanted us to be ready with an answer for questions about God. Peter knew that all of God's followers would be asked about their faith someday. Maybe someone has already asked you things like "Why do you believe in Jesus?" or "Why do you think God is real?"

The best way to be prepared for these questions is simply to tell your story about God's love. Has God forgiven you of your sin? Tell that story. Has Jesus helped you understand how to love others? That's a story you can tell too.

Jesus spent lots of time around people who asked

questions about Him. Many of them didn't believe He was God. Most of the time He responded with stories to help people understand God's love. You can do the same thing. When someone asks you about being a Christian, just tell your story! Tell them about God's love for you and why you follow Jesus.

KNOW AND DO!

- Ask an adult who loves God to help you practice telling your story.

- You can also share your favorite Bible verses. Memorize them and be ready to share them if someone asks. John 3:16 is a great one to start with!

Jesus Came for Everyone

Some Greek people had come to worship at the religious gathering. They were among the others who had come to worship. These Greek people came to Philip. He was from the city of Bethsaida in the country of Galilee. They said to him, "Sir, we want to see Jesus!"
John 12:20–21

––––––––––––––

There were many different people who followed Jesus—His twelve disciples, other men and women who were Jews like He was, and also people from other nations. Today's verse tells us that Greeks were following Jesus. Why does this matter? What does it mean for us today?

The Jews and the Greeks in Bible times did not always live together peacefully. They had different languages and religions, and they didn't look the same either. Rather than celebrate their differences and learn from each other, many of them hated each other. They were afraid of their differences. Sometimes they were even violent.

But Jesus brought the Jews and Greeks together. His love, His wisdom, His miracles—all of it was so amazing that even people who hated each other could agree about Jesus.

Our world is still divided. People fight with each other for terrible reasons—because they look different, or they're from different countries, or whatever. Rather than celebrate each other's differences, many people still react with fear and hatred.

But the good news that Jesus has paid the cost of sin *is for everyone*. Jesus didn't come just to save the Jews. He didn't come just to save the Greeks (and unless you are Jewish, you'd be a "Greek" in this verse). Jesus came to save everyone who will follow Him (Romans 10:9).

You can help spread the good news about Jesus by loving everyone, no matter where they come from or what they look like. Jesus loves them and you can too.

KNOW AND DO!

- Ask your parents about your great-grandparents. What country did they come from? What about your great-great-grandparents? You might be surprised!

- Memorize Galatians 3:28.

WATCH THE LIGHTNING

He makes the clouds rise from the ends of the earth.
He makes lightning come with the rain. He brings
the wind out from where He stores His riches.
PSALM 135:7

Buster is *the best* family dog. He's friendly and playful. He loves to chase frisbees and tennis balls. He doesn't bark too much. And he's always there for a hug when you're feeling sad.

But when there's thunder and lightning—watch out! Buster is scared of storms, and he'll sneak right by you to go hide. He will crawl under a bed and whimper until the storm has passed.

Thunderstorms can be frightening for people too. But Psalm 135 praises God for lightning! It reminds us that only God is strong enough to make storms and control the lightning. Only God can start and stop the weather.

Dogs like Buster need extra hugs to get them through a storm. Sometimes people do too. We can always remember that God controls the weather. We can praise Him for storms while we wait for the sunshine.

So when the lightning and thunder come, "praise the Lord, for the Lord is good" (Psalm 135:3).

KNOW AND DO!

- Lightning is a discharge—a release—of electro-static energy. It's similar to the shock you get when you rub your socked feet on the carpet, then touch a doorknob—but much, much bigger!

- The longest lightning bolt ever recorded was 321 miles long!

PUT YOUR HEAD IN THE CLOUDS

Ask the Lord for rain in the spring time. It is the Lord Who makes the storm clouds. He gives rain to men, and gives vegetables in the field to every one.
ZECHARIAH 10:1

"Get your head out of the clouds!"

Anne's teacher says this to her all the time. Why? Because Anne loves to daydream in class. She starts to imagine being somewhere else and pretty soon she has no idea what the lesson is about. "Get your head out of the clouds" is her teacher's way of saying, "Pay attention!"

In Bible times, a prophet named Zechariah had to remind Israel to pay attention too. They were tempted to worship false gods, forgetting the incredible differences between the real God and idols. So Zechariah used clouds to remind the people of God's power and love. Only the real God is able to send clouds and rain. Israel's animals and crops needed the rain to survive, and Israel needed the animals and crops to survive. Zechariah was saying, "Pay attention! Only the real God can feed us!"

Thank God for the clouds. Even if the day is gray, remember that clouds are another gift from God. They remind us of His love and power.

Next time you go outside, look up at the sky. What do the clouds look like? What do you see? Use your imagination! Put your head in the clouds!

KNOW AND DO!

- Have you ever wondered how many clouds are in the sky? Using satellites, scientists know that about half the earth is covered with clouds all the time. But it's impossible to know exactly how many clouds there are.

- Hundreds of years before Zechariah, God led Israel through a desert. Read about that in Exodus 13:21–22. How did God appear to the people?

GOD'S FOREVER LOVE

Give thanks to the Lord, for He is good,
for His loving-kindness lasts forever.
PSALM 136:1

———————

Many people say they *love* pizza. But after one meal, maybe two if you have leftovers, it's gone. There's nothing left to love.

Lots of kids say they *love* video games. But it's easy to get frustrated with games when they are hard to win. It's easy to get bored with an old game after a new game comes out. The love for the game is gone.

Some people say they *love* to go to movies. But soon the movie is over. Is the love gone?

What kind of love lasts?

The Bible says that *God's* love lasts forever. Not for a day or a month. Not sometimes, or only on weekends. God's love lasts *forever*.

Even when people make a bad choice?

Yup.

Even when people sin?

Double yup.

Even when the weather is bad, and the soda is flat, and the internet isn't working?

Triple yup.

God's love for you will never stop. It will never get weak or fade. Even when you're angry or tired or disobedient, God loves you. On good days and on bad days. When you're sick or healthy, when you're old or young, God's love endures forever.

Pizza, movies, and video games are all fun. But our love of these things is short compared to God's forever love. You do not ever have to wonder if you are loved. God's forever love surrounds you!

KNOW AND DO!

- Read Psalm 136:1–9 with your mom or dad and talk about what you've read.

- Who do you love? Mom? Dad? Grandma or Grandpa? Tell them how much you love them today!

BE A COMFORT BUILDER

*So comfort each other and make each
other strong as you are already doing.*
1 THESSALONIANS 5:11

Imagine that a woman wants to make her house taller. First, she makes sure the existing building is strong enough. She puts up new boards, drives nails into the thick wood, gets her house ready for the weight of the new rooms above. Later, when strong winds blow against the building, it won't fall down. It was built to be strong.

Words of *comfort* act the same way as the strong walls of a house. When we say kind things that comfort and encourage others, we build them up. They feel good about themselves. They feel confident and loved. If they're feeling sad, our comforting words will help them feel better more quickly.

But the opposite is true too. Unkind words tear people down—like a giant wrecking ball crashing into a building. Unkind words make people feel sad or angry.

So comfort others today! Say encouraging things. Tell your teachers how glad you are to be in their class. Give your parents a hug and say, "I love you." Find someone at school who looks sad and ask them how they are doing. Always look for ways to be a comfort builder!

KNOW AND DO!

- Say one comforting thing to your teacher, your bus driver, or your parents today. It will make a big difference!

- Read 1 Thessalonians 5:12–13. What should you do for those who work around you, especially at church?

Put Your Trust in Jesus

*"There are many rooms in My Father's house.
If it were not so, I would have told you. I am
going away to make a place for you."*
JOHN 14:2

Doug's house had three bedrooms. The first room belonged to his mom and dad. His two sisters shared the second room. Doug shared the third room with his two brothers. There were seven people in just three bedrooms. It was a full house! His parents eventually built more bedrooms in the basement so everyone could have more space.

Before Jesus died on the cross, He told His followers to "put your trust in Me" (John 14:1). He said He was going to heaven, but that He would come back for everyone who put their trust in Him. Jesus' followers didn't really understand. What did all this mean? Where was Jesus going?

Jesus described heaven as God's "house." He said there are "many rooms" in this house. That was His way of saying that heaven is big enough for everyone. Even big families, like Doug's, will have plenty of space to run and play in heaven.

"Putting your trust in Jesus" means that you believe Jesus is God's Son and that His death on the cross paid the cost of your sin. Have you put your trust in Jesus? If not, pray to God the Father. Tell Him you believe Jesus is His Son, and ask Him to forgive you of your sins. Then talk about it with your parents.

Nothing is more important than putting your trust in Jesus!

KNOW AND DO!

- If you have put your trust in Jesus today, write down the date so you won't forget it. This is a big day!

- Read about the way Jesus returned to heaven in Acts 1:9–11.

HIDE GOD'S WORD

Your Word have I hid in my heart,
that I may not sin against You.
PSALM 119:11

Tommy has a secret place to hide things. It's a small wooden box that his grandfather gave him. The box has a lid that closes with a metal latch and makes a satisfying *click* when it shuts. Inside the box are all Tommy's favorite things: His best trading cards in their plastic cases. A perfect seashell he found at the beach. A silver dollar coin. The foul ball he caught at a major league baseball game. Tommy keeps these things hidden away and protected because he cares so much about them. He wants to make sure they are always with him.

That's the idea we find in today's verse. What does it mean to "hide" God's Word in your heart? It means that you care as much about what God says as Tommy cares about his favorite things. It means you want to have God's Word close to you and part of your life.

We do this by spending time reading the Bible. We memorize our favorite verses. We think about those verses often, maybe even practice saying them when we wake up and before we go to bed. We let the words of God teach us how to live.

This is how you hide God's Word in your heart. Why not give it a try?

KNOW AND DO!

- Do you have a secret place for your favorite things? In the back of a drawer or under the bed? What kind of things do you like to save?

- Try to memorize a new verse this week. Write it down on a note card and keep it by your bed. Read the verse when you wake up. Read it again before you go to bed. Pray and ask God to "hide it in your heart."

Make Peace

*"Those who make peace are happy,
because they will be called the sons of God."*
MATTHEW 5:9

Do your brothers or sisters or friends argue a lot? Do they ever try to get you to join the argument too? Maybe they say things that they know will upset you, hoping you'll say something back.

Everyone argues now and then. Sometimes you have to argue, to stand up for what's right. There are cases when you have to fight to protect something important.

But most of the time, arguments can be avoided. Staying out of fights pleases God. Jesus taught His followers that God blesses "peacemakers," or those who do their best to keep people from arguing and fighting.

How can you be a peacemaker at home? Try sharing what you have with your siblings and not talking back to your mom or dad. When you're together, try to make sure everyone is comfortable and enjoying themselves. No matter what someone says to you—even if it's unkind—do your best to respond with gentle words and kindness.

How can you be a peacemaker at school or on the bus or on a team? The best way is to avoid arguments and fights in the first place. Don't join in! Instead, find an adult who can help solve the problem. And always choose to be a good example. Show your classmates and friends that problems can be solved without arguing.

When we live our lives like Jesus did—with love for other people—we will be peacemakers. We can share God's love by avoiding needless arguments. Make peace!

KNOW AND DO!

- Read Ephesians 4:3. Who will help you be a peacemaker?

- What could be better than a house full of delicious food? Read Proverbs 17:1 to find out.

Take Sin Seriously

"If your right eye is the reason you sin, take it out and throw it away. It is better to lose one part of your body than for your whole body to be thrown into hell. If your right hand is the reason you sin, cut it off and throw it away. It is better to lose one part of your body than for your whole body to go to hell."

Matthew 5:29–30

━━━━━━━━━━

"I'm so hungry I could eat a thousand pizzas," the boy said to his parents. "Well, I'm *starving*," his sister said. "I think I'm going to shrivel up and die if I don't eat soon." Mom and dad just smiled. These kids love to *exaggerate* when they're hungry.

Everyone exaggerates. It's one way we describe our thoughts and feelings: "She kicked that ball into the next county!" "I wish you didn't live a billion miles away!" "I love you so much I'm going to explode!"

Jesus was an amazing teacher. He taught people about God by telling stories, sometimes even with exaggeration. Today's verses are a good example. Does Jesus really want you to cut your hand off? No! Does He want you to poke your eye out? Not at all! So what are these verses really about?

Jesus was saying that we should do anything we need to do to avoid sin. Sin is a big deal—God takes it seriously, and so should we.

Everyone is tempted to sin at some time or another. We want to take things that aren't ours, or lie in order to hide something we've done wrong. There are lots of other things we could do that would hurt both God and us. So Jesus tells us to do our best to *avoid* sin.

Today, make the extra effort to live in ways that please God.

KNOW AND DO!

- Remember that God will always forgive you when you admit your sin! Read 1 John 1:9.
- In school you will learn the big word *hyperbole*. (It's pronounced hy-PUR-bowl-lee.) This word means exaggerating to make a point, like Jesus did.

Do It for the Lord

Whatever work you do, do it with all your heart. Do it for the Lord and not for men.
COLOSSIANS 3:23

Brian felt like he had so much work to do! In school, he was learning math, writing, reading, science, computers, and lots of other stuff he couldn't even remember. Then there was the homework. He hated homework! And then Brian's parents gave him chores: cleaning his room, taking out the garbage, and practicing the piano. Sometimes he even had to do the dishes.

It was all a lot of work. Would it ever stop? When would it be break time? Brian felt grumpy. He'd rather be playing. He was tempted to quit. . .or maybe to fake his working.

Have you ever been tempted like this? To not really clean your room, by just hiding the mess. Or to *sort of* finish your homework, making it just good enough to get by. At times, everyone is tempted to do things like this. What should we do when we don't feel like working?

The Bible tells us whenever we work, we should "do it for the Lord." That means our work—whatever we're doing—is a chance to show God our very best. Even if we'd rather be doing something else, we can show God that we are willing to put our desires on hold and do what we should do first.

When you work for the Lord, you'll even *enjoy* doing your best, because you know it's for God. Pleasing Him makes your work more fun. Whatever you do, do it for the Lord!

KNOW AND DO!

- Read Genesis 6:14–22—God's directions for Noah about how to build the ark. Try to draw a picture of it. . .and just imagine how much work Noah had to do!

- Think of some work you can do for a person you love. Then go and do it! This is one way to please God.

ENJOY GOD'S CREATION

*God made the big animals that live in the sea,
and every living thing that moves through the
waters by its kind, and every winged bird
after its kind. And God saw that it was good. . . .
Then God made the wild animals of the earth
after their kind, and the cattle after their kind,
and every thing that moves upon the ground after
its kind. And God saw that it was good.*
GENESIS 1:21, 25

———————————

Do you have an animal in your house? Do you wish you did?

Lots of people have a dog or a cat. Some keep guinea pigs or hamsters or goldfish. Depending on where you live, you might see squirrels or lizards outside. There are almost certainly bugs where you live and birds in the trees. Living creatures are everywhere!

Here's something to think about: God made all of those animals. The Bible tells us that every animal in the sea, every bird in the air, and every animal on land was made by God.

Brown-feathered robins with their delicate blue eggs were made by God. Playful puppies with their soft fur and wet tongues were made by God. Gulping goldfish with their wide eyes and shiny scales were made by God. The biggest, smelliest elephant in the zoo and the tiniest little bug on the playground—all these animals and so many more, all around the world, were made by God. They're amazing! And you know what? God thinks so too. The Bible tells us that after He created the animals, God "saw that it was good."

Animals are a wonderful part of nature. They're fun to learn about—and sometimes to play with. Animals show us how creative God is. He made kittens that cuddle and dogs that protect. He made eagles that soar through the clouds and whales that dive deep in the ocean. Each one reminds us of what God thinks is good. Look around and enjoy God's creation.

KNOW AND DO!

- Scientists have identified over 1.2 million different kinds of animals. Which is your favorite?

- The largest animal in the world is a blue whale, which can grow over 80 feet long. The smallest animal is a tiny frog, only 7.7 millimeters long. That's less than half as wide as a dime!

PRAISE

*Let everything that has breath
praise the Lord. Praise the Lord!*
PSALM 150:6

Ken loved his dog, Chance. Chance was always obedient and happy! Anything Ken said to do, Chance would do: "Come." "Sit." "Stay." "Jump!" "Roll over." Chance could do it all.

And Ken *praised* Chance: "You are such a good dog! Yes, you are! The sweetest puppy in the world!" Every time Ken praised the dog, Chance would wag his tail, harder and harder. Chance loved receiving praise.

What *is* praise? When you can't help but talk about how wonderful something is, that's praise. When you think someone is valuable, or important, or special—you praise that person by talking about him or her. You say all kinds of wonderful things about them.

Try praising *God* today. Do you love being outside in nature? Praise God for all you see, hear, and smell. Are you thankful for your family and friends? Praise God for the love you share together. Are you glad to know that God forgives us when we sin? Praise Him for His forgiveness. There are a million things to praise God for today. Give it a try!

KNOW AND DO!

- Psalm 150 lists several different instruments used to praise God. How does your Bible describe them?

- Do you play an instrument? If not, how about singing? Which song could you praise God with? Share with Him joyfully!

Meet Jonah

"But I will give gifts in worship to You with a thankful voice. I will give You what I have promised. The Lord is the One Who saves."
Jonah 2:9

Jonah's story is all about God's *mercy*. When God shows mercy, it means He does not give someone the punishment that he or she deserves.

God told Jonah to go to a city called Nineveh and share His love with the people there. Instead, Jonah ran away. He didn't want those people to follow God. Jonah thought they were wicked! And he didn't want God to show the Ninevites any mercy at all.

But you can't hide from God. (See Psalm 139:7–10 about that.) While Jonah was on a boat, trying to run away, God sent a big storm. Jonah was tossed into the sea, but he didn't drown. In His mercy, God sent a huge fish to *swallow* Jonah. That forced him to pray.

For three awful nights Jonah prayed inside that big, stinky fish. He prayed the words of today's verse. So God made the fish spit Jonah onto the beach. Before long, Jonah *did* go to Nineveh. Guess what? The people asked God to forgive them, and He did! God showed them mercy.

Jonah's story has some pretty strange parts, doesn't

it? The important thing is that it shows us God is merciful. Through Jesus, God offers mercy to people today. By your faith in Jesus, you can be saved from your sin.

Take a moment to think about God's mercy. He is "the One Who saves."

KNOW AND DO!

- Try reading the whole story of Jonah this week— it's only four chapters long.
- The stomach of a blue whale can hold up to *two tons* of food and water!

Thank God for All Things

*Always give thanks for all things to God the
Father in the name of our Lord Jesus Christ.*
EPHESIANS 5:20

Everyone has something to be thankful for. What did you have for breakfast? A cold glass of milk, some fruit, or maybe peanut butter and toast? Thank God for your food. Did a friend smile and say "Hi!" at school? Did a teacher give you a warm "Hello"? Thank God for your friends. Did someone in your family show you love today? A hug from mom or dad? A kiss on the cheek from Grandma? Thank God for your family.

Or maybe you can be thankful for something outside. Maybe you felt the wind on your cheeks or caught the smell of the grass in your nose. Maybe you heard the sound of birds today. Thank God for the world He created!

The Bible says to "always give thanks" to God—to thank Him for "all things." He created the beautiful earth. He gives us love, families, and friends. He gives us a fresh new day every morning. Each one is a chance to do things we love with the people we love.

We get so used to eating lunch and seeing trees that we forget they are gifts. We get so used to our moms, dads, grandparents, and friends, that we forget to thank God for them. So here's a reminder! What can you be thankful for today? Think about all the things you have enjoyed today. Think about all the people you got to talk to. Be sure to thank God for *all things*!

KNOW AND DO!

- Read Colossians 3:15. How often should we be thankful for God's gifts?

- God's greatest gift to us is Jesus, who paid the cost of our sin. His willingness to die for our sins is something to truly be thankful for. Thank God for Jesus!

KINGDOM OF GOD

*Jesus gave them another picture-story. He said,
"The holy nation of heaven is like yeast that
a woman put into three pails of flour until
it had become much more than at first."*
MATTHEW 13:33

When a baker makes cinnamon bread, she *rolls* the cinnamon into the dough. When the finished loaf is sliced, you can see spirals of that delicious brown cinnamon against the white of the bread. There's no missing this ingredient! If you baked the bread without the cinnamon, you would know right away. There would be no yummy-looking spirals when you sliced the loaf.

But there is an ingredient you can't see—it's called *yeast*. And the yeast is even more important than the cinnamon. After the bread is baked, the yeast is invisible. But it's the one ingredient that gives the loaf its shape. Yeast helps the bread puff up in the pan as it bakes. Without yeast, bread would be like a flat, hard cracker—no fun to eat.

Jesus compared the kingdom of God to yeast. What did He mean by that?

Well, when you follow God—praising Him, obeying Him, showing His love to others—you make a big difference in the world, the same way yeast makes a big difference in bread. Every decision you make to please God, even if no one else sees it, is important. Every bit of yeast, even if no one sees it, makes the bread fluffier and better.

Unlike the cinnamon, you can't see yeast—but it's a very important ingredient. The same is true of following God. That's the most important ingredient for life. . .for being part of God's kingdom.

KNOW AND DO!

- Jesus often talked about "the kingdom of God." When you love God and love others, you are living as a citizen of His kingdom.

- Yeast is a single-cell fungus. Can you believe a fungus helps make bread?

FOLLOW THE HARD ROAD

"Go in through the narrow door. The door is wide and the road is easy that leads to hell. Many people are going through that door. But the door is narrow and the road is hard that leads to life that lasts forever. Few people are finding it."
MATTHEW 7:13–14

———————

Jesus loved to teach about God by using examples that people were familiar with. One day He talked about following God by describing roads and doors. Jesus said that the road to "life that lasts forever" (being with God in heaven) is a hard road. The doorway to this road is "narrow," or hard to get through.

This means that following God is sometimes tough to do. Some days you might feel like it would be easier to lie than to tell the truth. Some days it might seem easier to focus on yourself rather than serve others. Sometimes, it's hard just to love certain people—especially when they don't love you back.

Jesus knows that following Him is not always easy. He wasn't afraid to say that, and you don't need to feel afraid to admit it. If you're struggling with some part of being a Christian, talk to Jesus about it in prayer. Tell Him why it's hard and ask for His help. You can also talk with a parent or someone else you love and trust. They will help you figure things out and stay faithful to God.

Jesus said the road of following Him is sometimes hard. But choosing to do what pleases God—even when it's difficult—is how we follow Jesus. Never forget that He loves you very much and will always be with you.

So stay on track. Follow the hard road.

KNOW AND DO!

- The first roads ever built were made of stone, thousands of years ago.

- To understand these verses better, imagine a big wide highway that your mom or dad drives on, compared to a narrow little pathway through a woods.

MEET RUTH

But Ruth said, "Do not beg me to leave you or turn away from following you. I will go where you go. I will live where you live. Your people will be my people. And your God will be my God."
RUTH 1:16

A high school student named Joanne loved her choir class. She told the teacher that she would always be there to help. Joanne showed up early to hand out music to other students. She also stayed to clean up the room after the others left. Joanne did whatever she could to help the teacher. She was committed.

When you make a commitment, you tell someone you will do something *and then you do it*. It's not always easy. Often, it takes hard work over a long period of time. One of the books in the Bible is about a young woman named Ruth and her mother-in-law, Naomi. It's all about *commitment*.

Ruth was married to Naomi's son. But then he died, around the time that Naomi's husband also died. As an older woman, Naomi was in a tough spot—women didn't usually have jobs, and now she had no man to provide for her needs.

But Ruth stepped up for Naomi. Even though she didn't have to, Ruth committed herself to her mother-in-law. Ruth was even willing to move to another country,

Naomi's homeland of Judah. They were poor, but Ruth worked hard to make sure she and Naomi had food to eat.

Eventually a man named Boaz noticed Ruth and committed himself to caring for her. He married Ruth and they had a son. This boy, Naomi's grandson, was a sign of God's commitment to the whole family. And in spite of all her losses, Naomi was able to find joy again.

This story happened thousands of years ago. But God has not changed. He is still committed to loving and caring for His people. The signs of His commitment might be the food you eat today, the love of your family and friends, or other things He gives you. Most of all, God shows His commitment by forgiving us of sin through Jesus.

So thank God for His commitment to you. Live out your commitments like Ruth did.

KNOW AND DO!

- The name *Ruth* means companion or friend.
- Who is your closest friend? Pray for him or her today.

Help Each Other

*Remember to do good and help
each other. Gifts like this please God.*
HEBREWS 13:16

The most embarrassing thing that ever happened to Grady was on the playground. Grady loved the tall metal swings. He would pump his legs until he was swinging so high he could see the whole playground. He loved the sound of the heavy chains and the feeling of the wind. *Clink. Whoosh! Clink. Whoosh!* Back and forth through recess.

The bell rang. Recess was over and it was time to line up by the doors. But on this day, something strange happened: While Grady was swinging, the metal hook at the end of the chain somehow got caught in his belt loop. When he tried to get off the swing, the hook pulled him backward by his pants. Grady slipped, twisted, and fell over! His shoulder hit the ground and his feet went up the air. His pants went up too! Grady's back was on the ground, his feet were tangled in the chain—and his underwear was showing.

No matter what Grady tried to do, he couldn't push himself up. He was stuck! And he was so embarrassed that he started to cry. A girl named Corinne recognized how upset Grady was, and she quickly helped him. She unhooked his belt loop from the chain and helped him stand up. Corinne didn't make fun of Grady or say anything that would embarrass him more. Then they ran together and lined up for class just in time.

Today's verse tells us that when we help each other, we please God. Corinne pleased God by helping Grady get unstuck. What can you do to help someone today? When you do, you will please God.

KNOW AND DO!

- Write down the names of three people you could help this week.

- Read Psalm 54:4. Who is your helper? What does this verse say He does for you?

TRUST THE LORD

"Good will come to the man who trusts in the Lord, and whose hope is in the Lord."
JEREMIAH 17:7

Natalie was so sad. Her family was getting ready to move from Massachusetts all the way to *Iowa*. She was in sixth grade and had a group of friends that she really liked. Iowa is really far away from Massachusetts! Natalie knew that it would be a long time before she saw her friends again. She'd have to start a new school and go to a new church.

After spending a whole Saturday packing her room, Natalie sat on her bed and cried. Her mom sat down beside Natalie, hugged her, and said, "Sweetheart, you have to trust me. Someday Iowa will feel like home. You will make new friends and you'll learn to fit in at your new school." All Natalie could do was trust her mom—to believe that what she said was true, even if it didn't always feel that way.

It's like this with God too. We don't always know how things are going to work out. We don't always know how God will provide the things we need. We just have to trust Him.

The great thing is that we can trust God with confidence! Think of all the stories you know about God— He provided Noah and his family with dry land after the flood; He saved Daniel from the lions' den; He has forgiven you of your sins through Jesus. These stories give us confidence in God. Whether you're moving across the country like Natalie or facing some other hard thing, you can trust God. He does not change. He always loves you and will provide for you.

Good will come to you when you trust the Lord!

KNOW AND DO!

- Psalm 7:1 is a prayer about trust in God. Why not try to memorize this verse?
- Who is one person you trust? Pray and thank God for that person.

The Lions' Den

Then the king was very pleased and had Daniel taken up out of the hole in the ground. So they took Daniel out of the hole and saw that he had not been hurt at all, because he had trusted in his God.
Daniel 6:23

If people lied about you and got you thrown into jail, would you still trust God? What if you weren't thrown into jail but into a pit of hungry lions? Then would you still trust God?

This is exactly what happened to Daniel.

Daniel was a Hebrew man who loved God. But he had been forced to live in a foreign country. Daniel worked for the king, and he was smart and good at his job. The king liked Daniel and wanted to give him even more power in the kingdom. But some of the other leaders hated Daniel. They didn't want him—someone from another country, a man who worshipped God—to get special treatment from the king. So they tricked the king into throwing Daniel into a lions' den for breaking the law! That was a punishment worse than jail—it meant instant death.

The king was so sad. Daniel would never survive! The lions had the power to crush and kill people, and they were used to punish only the most wicked people.

After a sleepless night the king ran to the lions' den

and called out, "Daniel, are you alive? Did your God protect you?"

"Yes! I'm alive!" Daniel shouted back. "God protected me because I trusted in Him." Daniel was lifted out of the den right away. There wasn't a scratch on him.

The king learned something about trusting in God: *He will do amazing things for those who trust Him.* Be like Daniel—trust in your God!

KNOW AND DO!

- What worries you? What makes you nervous or scared? Pray about it today and ask God to help you trust Him like Daniel did.

- Read all of Daniel 6 with your mom or dad. At the end of the story (verses 25–28), what did the king do after seeing Daniel's amazing trust in God? Then what else did the king do?

LOOK WITH ALL YOUR HEART

*"You will look for Me and find Me, when
you look for Me with all your heart."*
JEREMIAH 29:13

"You've got to look with your hands, Darnell. Go back and try again."

Darnell groaned as he turned back to the kitchen. He had been staring into the refrigerator for the last five minutes. He couldn't find the strawberry yogurt anywhere! All he wanted was to get a snack and go watch TV, but he couldn't find what he wanted. Each time he told his mom she would say the same thing: "You've got to look with your hands."

God says that you will find *Him* when you look "with all your heart." Your heart is your body's muscle for pumping blood. So what does it mean to *look* with your heart?

This verse is not about blood. But it is about something just as important: following God with everything you have. "Look with all your heart" is another way of saying "follow God with your full attention and your best energy." Looking with your heart means that you make your relationship with God the most important thing in your life.

Darnell's mom eventually helped him find the yogurt. "Look with your hands" means to move things around until you find what you're looking for. The yogurt was behind the milk—and when mom moved the milk, Darnell could see his snack.

You know, we can miss seeing God when we let other things become more important than Him. So make sure everything else is out of the way first. Look for Him with all your heart!

KNOW AND DO!

- An adult heart pumps about 2,000 gallons of blood a day!

- Read Jeremiah 29:13–14. These were God's words to His people, who had been taken from their homeland. What did He say He would do for His people after they found Him?

SHARE

*Share what you have with Christian brothers
who are in need. Give meals and a place
to stay to those who need it.*
ROMANS 12:13

───────────

Tyler really, really, really wanted to play video games after school. The problem was that his sister Madison really, really, really wanted to watch TV after school—and they only had one screen. Almost every day Tyler and Madison fought about who could use the TV. "It's my turn!" "No, it's not. You already had it!" "But you had it more yesterday." "Did not!" "Did too!"

Tyler and Madison just couldn't share. They fought so much that eventually their parents took the TV away completely. Neither of them would get to use it until they learned how to share with each another.

The apostle Paul wrote about sharing in the book of Romans. This "book" is actually a letter that Paul wrote to Christians in the city of Rome. They were having a hard time understanding what it means to follow Jesus. So Paul explained the good news about Jesus and what it means to live a life that pleases God. Paul told them to "share what you have," especially giving help to "those who need it."

Sharing is an important part of following Jesus. God shares with us—His love, forgiveness, and many other wonderful things—and He wants us to share with others. Sharing is one way to love other people, which pleases God.

So, what can *you* share today? Maybe some of your food or a favorite device? Your markers, your books, or your computer? Try to think of something you have that someone else could enjoy for a few minutes. It's good to share!

KNOW AND DO!

- If you were Tyler or Madison, what would you do?
- Romans is the longest letter of Paul in the Bible. Philemon is the shortest.

Be a Cheerful Giver

*Each man should give as he has decided in his heart.
He should not give, wishing he could keep it. Or he
should not give if he feels he has to give. God loves
a man who gives because he wants to give.*

2 Corinthians 9:7

———————

Madison had finally learned to share with her brother Tyler—sort of. Whenever she had to share with him, she would roll her eyes and say something rude. Share the TV after school? "*Fine.*" Cut the last cinnamon roll in half so they could each have a piece? "I guess if I *have* to." Let Tyler have the front seat in the car this time? "Whatever. I don't even care."

But the Bible tells us that God loves a *cheerful* giver. This means it's important to learn to share happily. Sharing because we have to may be following the rules, but God doesn't just care about rules. . .He cares about our hearts. God is asking us to share because we want to, not just because we have to. He wants us to see that sharing with others is more important than taking things for ourselves.

It took some time, but Madison eventually learned to share cheerfully with Tyler. She learned to stop using rude words, and instead spoke kindly to her brother.

It might take you some time too. But it's worth

learning! Sharing takes practice, so get started right away. It's possible—and wonderful—to be a cheerful giver!

KNOW AND DO!

- Read 2 Corinthians 9:11. Who gives you the things you have to share? Will you ever run out of things to give to others?

- What is one thing that would be hard for you to share? Why? Talk it over with your parents and pray about it together.

Faith in Bad Weather

After sending the people away, [Jesus' followers] took Jesus with them in a boat. . . . A bad wind storm came up. The waves were coming over the side of the boat. It was filling up with water. Jesus was in the back part of the boat sleeping on a pillow. They woke Him up, crying out, "Teacher, do You not care that we are about to die?" He got up and spoke sharp words to the wind. He said to the sea, "Be quiet! Be still." At once the wind stopped blowing. There were no more waves. He said to His followers, "Why are you so full of fear? Do you not have faith?" They were very much afraid and said to each other, "Who is this? Even the wind and waves obey Him!"
MARK 4:36–41

———————

One summer night a tornado got very close to a town full of people. The wind was so strong it cracked an old maple tree in half like a pencil. The big trunk fell toward a house—thankfully it landed on the porch, not the bedrooms. The family who lived in that house was afraid all night. But after the tornado was gone, they cleaned up the branches, praising God. He had saved them from the bad weather.

One time, Jesus' disciples were afraid of some bad weather too. It was evening, and they were in a boat on a small sea. Jesus was asleep in the back of the boat. Suddenly a storm blew up and started making big waves. The boat was filling with water! The disciples were afraid, and shaking Jesus awake, they shouted, "Don't You care that we're about to die?"

Jesus stood up and spoke in a stern voice: "Be quiet! Be still!" And the wind and the waves immediately calmed down. Then He said to the disciples, "Why are you so full of fear? Do you not have faith?"

At some point, everyone gets afraid of something. But the disciples' fear made them doubt the love of Jesus. Instead of saying, "Let's have faith in Jesus; go wake Him up," they shouted, "Don't you care?" Of course Jesus cared—and He still cares now.

When something scary is happening, you *can* count on God. He *does* care. You can have faith in *any* kind of weather.

KNOW AND DO!

- Do you remember what faith means? For a reminder, re-read Hebrews 11:1 and the devotion "Faith" (page 29).

- Why were the disciples in a boat? Read Mark 4:1 for the answer.

Meet an Eight-Year-Old King

Josiah was eight years old when he became king.
And he ruled thirty-one years in Jerusalem.
He did what was right in the eyes of the Lord,
and walked in the ways of his father David.
He did not turn aside to the right or to the left.
2 Chronicles 34:1–2

———————

What if you could be a king or queen when you were *eight* years old? What amazing things would you do with your power and money? Buy thousands of toys and rooms full of candy? Go to a theme park every weekend? Well, the Bible tells the story of a real eight-year-old king and the amazing things he did. His name was Josiah.

As king, Josiah removed false gods—called *idols*—from the land. He destroyed the places where those idols were worshipped, and he removed the false religious leaders too. Why did he do that? Because the idols and false teachers were preventing people from growing close to the real God, the Creator who loved them very much.

But these good decisions aren't all that makes Josiah special. He is super special because he chose to serve God at a young age. And that made a big difference for the adults around him—for his whole country!

You may never be a king or queen, but your decision to follow God can make a big difference too. Loving your family and friends—and forgiving them when they say or do bad things—will make a difference. This is a great way to serve God. Praying to God and praising Him every day is another way to live like Josiah did. Even adults will notice these things.

You can make a big difference. Follow God with all your heart!

KNOW AND DO!

- See what Josiah did when he became king in 2 Chronicles 34:1–7. Even children can make big changes when they obey God!

- Read 1 Timothy 4:12. Children who love God can be an example to anyone—even adults!

SHARE YOUR GIFTS

*God has given each of you a gift. Use it to help
each other. This will show God's loving-favor.*
1 PETER 4:10

A woman named Yvonne has played the piano in church since she was a little girl. Now she's in her eighties, but she still plays every week.

Yvonne is good at working with the other musicians too. She picks out music, leads rehearsals, and plays for the choir. She's more than just a piano player—Yvonne is someone her community depends on. Church leaders rely on her to make sure the music is good each week. People in the church would miss Yvonne badly if she decided not to play anymore. They count on her and they don't even realize it!

A long time ago Yvonne learned today's verse. She believes that God gave her the musical talent she has. Now she loves to give music back to God—and to her whole community.

God has given you gifts too. You might not know what they are yet, but you do have some. As you grow, your gifts and talents will appear. Like branches that stretch wide and strong from a tree trunk, your talents will become plain to everyone. And today's verse says you should use your gifts to help others. When you do, you show God's grace to other people.

Your gift is like a light behind a closed door. Open that door, and light spills into the darkness and welcomes people in. As soon as you discover your gifts, share them with others!

KNOW AND DO!

- One of God's gifts to us is *grace*—love and blessings we don't deserve because of sin. It's a wonderful gift!

- Read Romans 12:6–10. What must be sincere or true when we share our gifts?

HOT STUFF

"If we are thrown into the fire, our God Whom we serve is able to save us from it. And He will save us from your hand, O king. But even if He does not, we want you to know, O king, that we will not serve your gods or worship the object of gold that you have set up."
DANIEL 3:17–18

Can you imagine a fire so hot it would kill you just to be near it? Can you imagine a furnace so big that you and three others could walk around inside it? The Bible tells a story about a huge, fiery furnace, one so hot it killed some men who got close to it. But in this horrible place, God did something incredible.

In a place called Babylon, three followers of God—Shadrach, Meshach, and Abed-nego—refused to worship an idol. They would only give their love and praise to the true God. The king of Babylon was so angry that he decided to kill the young men by throwing them into the furnace. But God saved them. Shadrach, Meshach, and Abed-nego walked through the incredible heat unburned, as if the flames weren't even there!

But why did God even allow them to be thrown into the furnace? Why not save them before they were in the flames?

The Bible tells us that the miracle God performed helped the king of Babylon to understand God in a brand-new way. The king realized "there is no other god who is able to save in this way" (Daniel 3:29).

And that is true of God today! He still saves people—from sin. Others will understand God in a brand-new way when they see the miracle He does in our lives. So worship Him, like Shadrach, Meshach, and Abed-nego did. And watch what miracles He makes happen!

KNOW AND DO!

- There was a fourth person in the furnace when God performed this miracle. Read Daniel 3:25 to learn who it was.

- Not all flames are the same temperature. They range from about 1,100 degrees to nearly 6,000 degrees!

The Safe Place

*God is our safe place and our strength. He is
always our help when we are in trouble.*
Psalm 46:1

Carson Dooley was the oldest child in a loving family. He
had little brothers and sisters who looked up to him. His
parents loved him like crazy too. So when doctors told
them that Carson had cancer, it was like their world was
going dark. Many scary questions came to their minds:

Will Carson live through the cancer?

Will Carson get to grow up?

*Will the other kids understand what's happening to their
big brother?*

Carson's parents couldn't answer any of these questions right away. All they could do was pray and trust God.

Psalm 46 is a wonderful chapter to read when it
feels like the world is going dark. The psalm reminds us
that God is our "safe place" and our "strength"—and that
we don't need to be afraid when bad things happen because "He is always our help when we are in trouble."
The Dooley family trusted God while Carson was in the
hospital. It was hard, but they knew that God could give
them strength to face each difficult day.

When bad things happen, we all have questions. Like
the Dooley family, we are surprised by bad news—and
we want answers. Today's verse reminds us that, even if

we don't have answers, we can count on God's strength and help. He is our safe place.

KNOW AND DO!

- When this psalm was written, safe places were also called fortresses. A fortress is a strong, long-lasting place, one that is safe from attackers.

- Does something in your life make you feel weak? Pray to God, asking Him for strength to face it.

A SCAR'S STORY

[Jesus] said to Thomas, "Put your finger into My hands. Put your hand into My side. Do not doubt, believe!" Thomas said to Him, "My Lord and my God!"
JOHN 20:27–28

Kevin was carrying a heavy box up the staircase. The old carpet on the stairs was smashed down and slippery, and his worn-out tennis shoes didn't have much traction.

"Oops!" Kevin yelled as his foot slipped. He almost fell backward, but at the last second, Kevin leaned into the wall to stop his body from falling.

Then another yell: "Ouch!" There was a nail in the wall where a picture frame had once hung. When Kevin's hand smashed into the nail's head, it poked a hole in his skin that left a scar the size of an M&M. Many years later, Kevin still has the scar as a reminder of how he almost fell down the stairs.

Did you know that, after Jesus rose from the dead, He had scars? The Bible says that the nails used to hang Him on the cross left marks in His hands. And that the spear that pierced His side left a hole. One disciple, Thomas, said he wouldn't believe Jesus was alive again unless he saw those scars.

Why? Scars tell a story. They are proof that some painful wound has been healed. The holes in Jesus' hands and side tell the story of His death on the cross to pay for our sin. But the story doesn't end there. His scars show that His painful wounds are healed. He is alive today!

Jesus told Thomas, "Do not doubt. Believe!" We can do the same. Know your Bible to the story His scars tell: Jesus was dead, but now He is alive!

KNOW AND DO!

- Do you have a scar on your arm or leg? What story does it tell?
- You can read the full story of the disciple Thomas in John 20:19–31.

GIVE GOD YOUR WORRIES

*Give all your worries to Him
because He cares for you.*
1 PETER 5:7

Angelo worried about things. He worried about sleeping through his alarm clock and being late for the bus. When his family ordered pizza for dinner, he worried that he would get the smallest piece. When he played with toys with his brothers, he worried that the toys would get lost or broken. He worried so much he could hardly have any fun. Worry often made Angelo unhappy.

The Bible tells us to give (or "cast") our worries to God. It's like we throw them to Him. We don't just ask God quietly to help us with our worries—we grab hold of all our worried feelings and throw them to God in prayer.

This is the same God who saved Daniel from the lions. The same God who stopped the flood and led Noah to dry land. The same God who helped young David defeat a giant warrior. We can trust that God is big enough and strong enough to catch all our worries and take them away.

Have you ever done this? Have you ever prayed and said, "God, I'm so worried about something. Would You help me to trust You? Would You take these worries away?"

What are you worried about today? It doesn't matter

how big or small your worries are. Pray right now and "cast" them to God. You can trust Him!

KNOW AND DO!

- Jesus talked about worry in Matthew 6:25–34. Read the verses to see what He said.

- Worry distracts us from what God is doing in our lives. Take a minute and try to name five great things in your life. Focus on these things instead of your worries.

Follow God's Path

Trust in the Lord with all your heart, and do not trust in your own understanding. Agree with Him in all your ways, and He will make your paths straight.
PROVERBS 3:5-6

———————

Most phones have apps that give directions. Have you seen your mom or dad use one while they're driving? They are very helpful! You type in the address you need to find, and the app shows you how to get there. If the path is blocked for some reason, the app will even give you directions for a new path.

Today's verse is about trusting God instead of "your own understanding." This means that sometimes God will give you directions to do something, but you won't understand why. You might feel like He wants you to help someone out, but you just finished your homework—don't you get any time for yourself? Or maybe you feel like God wants you to pray for someone at school, but that person is really mean—why would you pray for her?

God knows things that we don't know, and He asks us to trust Him.

The great thing is that we can count on God to "make our paths straight." That means He will lead us to do things that please Him and show love to others. Will you always get to do what you want? No—sometimes you have to give up your personal time to help someone else.

But God knows best, and when we do the best things, we find that they make us happy.

Follow God's path. . .and find real happiness.

KNOW AND DO!

- The next verse after today's scripture has a clue for following God's paths: "Turn away from what is sinful."

- Can you think of someone who needs prayer today? Ask God to bless that person.

See the Work of God

Jesus answered, "The sin of this man or the sin of his parents did not make him to be born blind. He was born blind so the work of God would be seen in him."
JOHN 9:3

———————

Grandpa J. B. was very old. He wasn't very healthy either. His eyesight was weak, and his knee was bad. It was hard for him to move around or do very much. It seemed like he was always visiting the doctor because of some new problem. But when his grandsons came to visit, they found Grandpa J. B. joyful and thankful for life. He told them, "It hurts to walk because of my knee, and I can't see like I used to, but these problems make me lean on God even more! Every day I thank Him for the things I *can* see and the things I *can* do. Every day I'm reminded of how much God must love me, and then I love Him more too."

In today's verse, Jesus healed a blind man. This man who had been born without eyesight was suddenly able to see (John 9:1–7). Imagine how incredible that must have been!

Then the disciples asked Jesus why the man had been born blind. Jesus said it was "so the work of God would be seen in him." Because of that blindness, many people learned about Jesus (John 9:8–12).

This is the way Grandpa J. B. thought about his bad

eyes and knee. "These problems make me lean on God even more!" He didn't ask God why his health was bad—he just looked for the work of God in his life. That's something we can all do.

KNOW AND DO!

- There were religious leaders—Pharisees—who did not believe Jesus was God's Son. Read their story in John 9:13–34. Do you think they were leaning on God?

- Jesus seemed to enjoy healing the blind. Look at Luke 7:21.

WORSHIP

Christian brothers, I ask you from my heart to give your bodies to God because of His loving-kindness to us. Let your bodies be a living and holy gift given to God. He is pleased with this kind of gift. This is the true worship that you should give Him.
ROMANS 12:1

―――――――――

Church was a little confusing for Katie. She didn't really understand what *worship* was.

Every Sunday Katie's family went to a "worship service." They passed the offering plates as an "act of worship." Their church even has a "worship pastor," a "worship band," and "worship music." But no one told Katie what worship actually means. Do you know?

If you worship someone, you show honor and respect to that person above anyone else. Worshipping God can be telling Him how much you love Him in a prayer, singing songs about Him, or even just trusting Him.

An "act of worship" is taking something you have and offering it to God. When the people at Katie's church put money in the offering plate, or when someone gives their time to help a person in need, these are acts of worship. Avoiding sin—not doing some bad thing you want to do—is an act of worship. Obedience to God— giving Him your desires and time, rather than saving them for yourself—is an act of worship too.

Try to worship God today. Your acts of worship help you grow closer to Him. They'll remind you of all the good things you know about God—that He loves you, that He has forgiven you of sin, and that He's a promise keeper. Pray and thank Him, sing a song about Him, or serve Him by helping another person. There are so many reasons and ways to worship God!

KNOW AND DO!

- Psalm 22:27–28 says that, someday, many nations will worship God. How many?
- How does Revelation 15:4 compare with Psalm 22:27–28?

FIND SOMETHING
BETTER THAN GOLD

*Happy is the man who finds wisdom, and the
man who gets understanding. For it is better
than getting silver and fine gold.*
PROVERBS 3:13–14

———

Have you ever seen a golden ring? Many couples give each other gold rings when they get married. That yellow gold shines like sunlight on water! Maybe you've seen your grandma wear a gold necklace or gold earrings. Maybe you've seen gold treasure in a movie or read about it in a book. Gold is one of the most valuable and beautiful metals on earth. With enough gold you would be rich! What could be better than gold?

The Bible tells us that *wisdom* is better than gold. But how? You can't buy a new phone with wisdom. You can't pay for video games or clothes with wisdom. How could it be worth so much?

Wisdom is the ability to make good decisions in all kinds of situations—decisions that please God.

Some people think that to be wise, you have to be super smart. But being wise is not about how smart you are. There are many *smart* people who are not *wise* because they use their knowledge for selfish things. A wise person will use all that they have to love God and other people.

Do you want to find something worth more than gold? Find wisdom! Read the Bible and share the good news about Jesus. Show others the same love and kindness that God has shown you. This is how you will find wisdom. Go for it!

KNOW AND DO!

- You don't need to be old to be wise. Re-read "Meet an Eight-Year-Old King" (page 167) to discover a child who was wise.

- Read James 1:5. How can you get wisdom?

REPENT

*"I tell you, there will be more joy in heaven
because of one sinner who is sorry for his sins and
turns from them, than for ninety-nine people right
with God who do not have sins to be sorry for."*
LUKE 15:7

Here's something a wise person has said: *Sin never seems
as bad as it really is until we have to tell someone about it.*
If you cheat on a test and no one catches you, it seems
like it's not that big of a deal. If you steal a snack when
no one is looking, well, who cares? It was just a snack. Or
maybe you tell a "little white lie" in order to get your way.
You don't feel too guilty as long as no one knows.

But what about when you get caught? Then you feel
terrible. You don't want to admit what you've done. You
might cry or get mad. That's because we understand how
bad sin really is when we talk it about it with someone
else. It's like bringing some ugly thing out of the dark and
into a bright light.

When we sin, we're drifting away from God. Sin distracts us from the good path, the same way a sheep wan-
ders away from its flock and gets lost in the wilderness.
But Jesus is our shepherd and He wants us back on the
path back to God. How can we return to Him?

By *repenting*. That means turning from your sin and
toward God. Pray and tell God you're sorry for your sin.

When you repent, the shepherd hears and comes to bring you back home.

Do you know what the best part is? God *loves* it when we repent! Today's verse tells us that whenever a sinner repents there is rejoicing in heaven! So jump in to repentance and leave your sins behind.

KNOW AND DO!

- Read Jesus' story about the lost sheep in Luke 15:3–7.

- Don't be afraid to talk to God about sin! He will always listen and forgive you.

TURN BACK TO GOD

*"For my son was dead and now he is alive again.
He was lost and now he is found. Let
us eat and have a good time."*
LUKE 15:24

———

Jesus told many parables, like yesterday's story about the sheep and the shepherd. Each story was used to explain something about God or His kingdom. Many consider Jesus to be a master storyteller.

Another of Jesus' parables is about an incredibly loving dad. This dad had a selfish son who basically said, "Dad, I'm leaving! Give me all the money I would get if you died. I want to party." The father was heartbroken but did as his son asked.

Time passed. The son wasted all of his dad's money on parties and worthless things. Before long, he was broke, he had no friends, and he had nowhere to go. He decided to return home.

The young man expected his dad to be really angry— to treat him as if they weren't even related. But this dad loved his son more than that! He saw the young man coming up the road and ran out to meet him. The dad hugged his boy and shouted with joy to the neighbors: "My son has come home! My son has come home!"

Jesus told this story so people would understand God's love. When someone turns away from sin and back to God—when they *repent*—He is like the dad in Jesus' story. He runs to meet whoever returns home, hugging them and laughing and shouting with joy.

God loves you, deeply and wildly. No matter what you've done, and no matter what has been done to you, He is waiting to see you again. Whenever you find yourself unhappy and alone, turn back to God!

KNOW AND DO!

- There are actually two sons in Jesus' story. What can you learn from the other one? Read Luke 15:11–32.

- Have you ever done something you feel ashamed about? Talk with God about it in prayer. No matter what you've done, His love for you is like the dad's in this story.

RESPOND TO GOD

Then the Lord came and stood and called as He did the other times, "Samuel! Samuel!" And Samuel said, "Speak, for Your servant is listening."
1 SAMUEL 3:10

When Sue went to the hospital, her friend Gretchen wanted to do something to help. She prayed and prayed that God would make Sue get better. That's when Gretchen got the idea to have everyone in their class make special get-well cards. It was a wonderful idea that made Sue feel loved.

When Steve moved into the neighborhood, Kevin felt like God wanted him to be a friend. So at the bus stop Kevin introduced himself and offered to let Steve sit with him on the ride to school. Kevin kept thinking about a verse he had memorized in church: "Do for other people whatever you would like to have them do for you" (Matthew 7:12). He just knew it was the right thing to do.

Today's verse is about a boy named Samuel whom God called to become a prophet—someone who spoke for God to Israel. Samuel obeyed and became an important part of God's story. But God didn't wait until Samuel was grown up. God called Samuel as a child.

God still asks children to do His work. You may not hear God speak out loud, but He prompts people to do good things through His Holy Spirit. Kevin felt God call him through the Bible verse he memorized. Gretchen felt God call her after she prayed.

If you think God might be asking you to do something, respond like Samuel did. Say, "Speak, for Your servant is listening." Then get started!

KNOW AND DO!

- If you're not sure if God is asking you to do something, talk to an adult and pray together.

- Samuel set up two of Israel's kings by "anointing" them—pouring oil on their heads to show people they'd been chosen. Which kings? Read 1 Samuel 10:1 and 16:11–13 to find out.

SHOW YOUR HEART

But the Lord said to Samuel, "Do not look at
the way he looks on the outside or how tall he is,
because I have not chosen him. For the Lord does
not look at the things man looks at. A man looks at
the outside of a person, but the Lord looks at the heart."
1 SAMUEL 16:7

Lewis was an ordinary boy. He liked chocolate donuts, a cold glass of milk, and watching cartoons on Saturday morning. He loved his parents and had a lot of fun with his brothers and sisters at home. But at school, things were different. Some kids made fun of Lewis for the way he looked. Some said his clothes weren't cool. Others said his hair was weird. One guy said Lewis should get a new backpack. Lewis felt like he could never be good enough.

Have you ever felt this way—like everyone was judging you for the way you look rather than for who you are? There is good news! God will *never* do that to you.

Today's verse tells about the time the prophet Samuel anointed young David to be Israel's future king. David had many more impressive older brothers. Their muscles were as big as boulders. They were fighters and soldiers. David was "just" a shepherd boy—a kid who smelled like the animals he cared for all day long. But God told Samuel that "the Lord looks at the heart."

You can't stop other kids from judging you. But you

can trust in God's judgment. He looks at your heart. He sees what you care about and how you treat others. He watches how you respond to Him. When you remember that God loves you for who you are inside, what other people say doesn't matter. You gain confidence to let other people's judgment just fall away.

Show your heart to God. . .He cares about who you are *inside*.

KNOW AND DO!

- Samuel met seven of David's impressive brothers before God chose David (1 Samuel 16:10–11)!

- As an adult, David asked God to clean his heart of sin. Read Psalm 51:10.

COMPASSION

[Jesus] said to them, "Give them something to eat."
They said to Him, "Are we to go and buy many loaves of
bread and give it to them?" He said to them, "How many
loaves of bread do you have here? Go and see." When
they knew, they said, "Five loaves of bread and two fish."
MARK 6:37–38

Kristen felt so sad when she saw the bird on the ground. Its wing was twisted, and its silky feathers were torn. It was lying in the grass under a tree rather than sitting in the branches. It was obviously hurt, so Kristen decided to take it to a veterinarian right away. She just couldn't let it lie there alone.

On a day when Jesus wanted to be alone with His disciples, over 5,000 people were following Him around. They were hungry to learn about God—so hungry that they forgot to bring something to eat. Then their stomachs got hungry too!

So Jesus asked the disciples, "How much food do you have for these people?" Their answer was just five loaves of bread and two fish—that's a lunch for one person, not thousands! But Jesus performed a miracle. After praying, He started to break the food into pieces and hand it to the disciples. They gave it to the people as Jesus kept breaking and breaking and breaking that food. By God's power, that small lunch never ran out.

Jesus' miracles don't always make sense. How could such a tiny amount of food feed so many people? But figuring out how God works isn't the point of this story. It's why Jesus did what He did—because He had *compassion*.

Jesus was aware of the people's needs, and He wanted to help them. This is compassion. He knew they were hungry, both for God and for food. So He taught them and He fed them.

Have you ever felt like one of those people? Like you are far from God and hungry to be close again? Thank God for His compassion. . .and let Jesus perform a miracle in your life too.

KNOW AND DO!

- Is there someone you want to help today? Can you practice compassion today?

- After Jesus performed this miracle, how much food was left over? Read Mark 6:43.

You Are God's Work

*We are His work. He has made us to belong
to Christ Jesus so we can work for Him.
He planned that we should do this.*
EPHESIANS 2:10

———

Have you ever heard of a *luthier*? That is someone who builds and repairs stringed instruments—like acoustic guitars, violins, and cellos. Luthiers carefully reshape wood (making sure they don't crack it), glue it in place, and sand it smooth in order to make their instruments.

An *architect* is a person who designs homes, offices, and other buildings. Architects are good at math, computers, and working with tools. They understand what people need in their homes and offices, and they develop creative ways to make useful buildings.

A *sculptor* is an artist who creates statues out of rock, clay, or other materials. Sculptors are able to imagine a work of art inside a hunk of other material. And they're willing to spend the time necessary to bring out that artwork.

Each of these people gives us a glimpse into what God is like. The first chapter of the Bible, Genesis 1, tells us He created the natural world—from the farthest asteroid in space to the tiniest fish swimming in the ocean. God is careful like a luthier, understanding and creative like an architect, and able to see the potential in people like a sculptor.

The best part? *You* are one of God's good works. You are not an accident. You were made on purpose and God loves you very much. That's a reason to praise your Creator today!

KNOW AND DO!

- Today's verse says we were made "to belong to Christ Jesus so we can work for Him." Pray and ask God to show you how to work for Him.

- Do you know people who create things? Ask them to tell you how they learned to do what they do.

BE KIND AND COMPASSIONATE

You must be kind to each other. Think of the other person. Forgive other people just as God forgave you because of Christ's death on the cross.
EPHESIANS 4:32

Robert watched from the other room as his older brother got in *big* trouble. Robert couldn't believe it—his brother had stolen something from a store and got caught! Their parents were so angry. Robert hid in the shadows of the hallway, listening to the whole conversation.

This is perfect! Robert thought. His brother was always pushing him around, making fun of Robert for being younger. But this time, *Robert* could be the one making fun. His brother had made a big mistake and Robert was never going to let him forget it.

That night, when his brother crawled into his bed on the other side of their bedroom, Robert was just about to say, "Ha, ha! You got in trouble!" But then he heard something he hardly ever heard—his older brother was crying.

God tells His children to be kind and compassionate to others. In His own kindness and compassion, God has forgiven all of us of countless sins. He wants us to treat others the same way.

His brother's crying made Robert realize how ashamed and sorry he must have felt. In that moment, Robert made a decision. Instead of taking the opportunity to make fun, he showed kindness. In the dark bedroom Robert said, "It's okay, bro. Mom and Dad are upset, but they love you. They'll calm down. Everything will be fine soon."

Simple words of kindness and compassion are amazingly powerful. Share them with others.

KNOW AND DO!

- In this story, Robert's brother wasn't the only person helped. Had Robert been mean, he would have felt ashamed of himself before long. Kindness helped him too.

- Who can you be kind to today?

JESUS CHANGES LIVES

"For the Son of Man came to look for and to save from the punishment of sin those who are lost."
LUKE 19:10

Every spring, people across the United States file their tax returns. This means people show the government records of the money they made over the past year, as well as the taxes they have already paid. If they have paid more than they needed to, the government refunds (gives back) the extra money. If they haven't paid enough, the government expects a payment. Tax returns are not much fun—they're sort of like a boring homework assignment. (Ask your parents.) But "doing taxes" is a normal part of American life.

It was different in the time of Jesus. People called tax collectors went around demanding payment. They were well known to be thieves and liars. They forced people to overpay their taxes, and then they would keep the extra money for themselves. Tax collectors had few friends and lots of enemies. No one wanted to be seen with them.

But a tax collector named Zaccheus wanted to change his life, and Jesus knew it. When He entered Zaccheus' town Jesus said, "I must stay in your house today" (Luke 19:5), even though that made everyone grumble. Why? Because Jesus came to save everyone, even thieves and liars. Jesus didn't really care what other people thought.

It was more important to Him that Zaccheus understood God's love.

Praise God that He cares for every person! Zaccheus' life was changed after meeting Jesus. Has yours been changed too? Thank God!

KNOW AND DO!

- Zaccheus is famous for being short and climbing a tree to see Jesus. Read the whole story in Luke 19:1–10.

- Do you know someone who lies and steals? Do you know someone who is mean? Will you pray for that person?

JESUS IS ALIVE

[The angel] said, "Do not be afraid. You are looking for Jesus of Nazareth Who was nailed to a cross. He is risen! He is not here! See, here is the place where they laid Him."
MARK 16:6

———————

Imagine you just ate at a restaurant—but you don't have money to pay for the food. When the bill comes due, the manager might make you work to pay the cost of what you ate. She might have you clean dishes or wipe down tables. Now imagine that a friend volunteers to do the work for you, even though he didn't eat. That friend pays the cost of the food in your place.

In a very small way, that pictures why Jesus let Himself be killed on the cross. The debt He paid was much, much worse than a restaurant bill! Jesus paid the debt of sin by giving His life. It was the only way to cover the cost (Romans 6:23).

But the story didn't end when Jesus died. Three days later, He came back to life. This is called *resurrection*. Jesus' resurrection from death started a new chapter in God's story. After the resurrection, Jesus' disciples finally began to understand that God wants to save *all* people from sin and death—and that faith in Jesus is how He does that.

The resurrection of Jesus fills us with hope! We know that God is more powerful than anything—even death. Years later the apostle Paul would say that God "made us alive by what Christ did for us. . . . God raised us up from death when He raised up Christ Jesus" (Ephesians 2:5–6).

You can worship Jesus because *He is alive*! Sin and death could not keep Him in the grave! As the angel said that day, "He is risen! He is not here!"

KNOW AND DO!

- Read 1 Corinthians 15:3–8. These verses tell about all the people who saw Jesus after His resurrection.

- Does death seem scary? How does Jesus' resurrection make things better?

READ THE ENDING

*Then the angel showed me the river of the water of life.
It was as clear as glass and came from the throne of God
and of the Lamb. It runs down the center of the street
in the city. On each side of the river was the tree of life.
It gives twelve different kinds of fruit. It gives this fruit
twelve times a year, new fruit each month. Its leaves
are used to heal the nations. There will be nothing in the
city that is sinful. The place where God and the Lamb
sit will be there. The servants He owns will serve Him.*
REVELATION 22:1–3

The best movies have great endings. The music swells.
There are explosions and battles. The good guys blow up
the enemy base. The hero defeats the deadly villain. The
world is saved and things return to normal. And there is
usually at least one prince and princess who fall in love.

Okay, not every story has explosions or princesses.
But a good story needs a good ending.

You can think about the Bible as one big story that re-
veals God. When you read the books of the Bible, you will
see how God acts, what He thinks, and what He wants for
you. Best of all, you'll see what He has done to show you
His love. This story has a great ending too.

The last two chapters in the Bible, Revelation 21 and
22, are the Bible's great ending. They give us a glimpse
of a time when God has removed all the sin and evil from

the earth. This incredible vision describes a place that is full of light and peace, a place where God is loved and worshipped by everyone.

Right now, you are probably in the early part of God's story for your life. You might be facing villains or fighting battles of your own. Life isn't always easy. But followers of God can find hope in the ending of God's story. Jesus will return to earth someday. He will destroy sin and evil for good. He will make everything right.

Know your Bible—and praise God for the awesome ending to His story!

KNOW AND DO!

- Is anything bothering you right now? Can you pray about this "battle"?

- What does Jesus say three times in Revelation 22? Read verses 7, 12, and 20.

ANOTHER GREAT BOOK FOR KIDS!

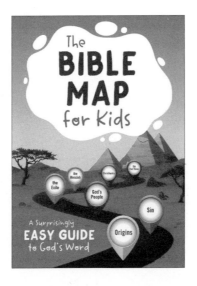

This surprisingly easy guide walks you through seven "lands" of scripture: Origins, Sin, God's People, the Exile, the Messiah, Christianity, and the End Times. Each one is plainly described and set into the big picture of God's love for you!

Paperback / 978-1-63609-564-6